EDITOR: LEE JOHNSON

WARRIOR SERIES 8

BRITISH CAVALRYMAN
1792–1815

Text by
PHILIP HAYTHORNTHWAITE
Colour plates by
RICHARD HOOK

First published in Great Britain in 1994 by
Osprey Publishing,
Michelin House, 81 Fulham Road,
London SW3 6RB
© Copyright 1994 Osprey Publishing Ltd.
Reprinted 1998

ISBN 1 85532 364 8

Filmset in Great Britain by Keyspools Ltd.
Printed through World Print Ltd, Hong Kong

Acknowledgements
The author extends especial thanks to Dr. John A.
Hall, and to Alan Harrison.

Artist's Note
Readers may care to note that the original paintings
from which the colour plates in this book were
prepared are available for private sale. All
reproduction copyright whatsoever is retained by the
publisher. Enquiries should be addressed to:
  Scorpio Gallery
  PO Box 475
  Hailsham
  E. Sussex BN27 2SL.
The publishers regret that they can enter into no
correspondence upon this matter.

Publisher's Note
Readers may wish to study this title in conjunction
with the following Osprey publications:
  MAA 126 *Wellington's Light Cavalry*
  MAA 130 *Wellington's Heavy Cavalry*
  MAA 138 *British Cavalry Equipments 1800–1941*
  Campaign 15 *Waterloo 1815*

INTRODUCTION

In the campaigns of the French Revolutionary and Napoleonic Wars, the deserved reputation of the British infantry has tended to overshadow the contribution of the cavalry. The army's mounted branch was not large: reckoning rank and file only, and excluding artillery, in 1794 the cavalry represented 17 per cent of the army (14,527 men out of 85,097), rising to 23 per cent by 1795 (28,810 out of 124, 262). After the renewal of the war in 1803 the percentage declined: 12.5 per cent in 1805 (20,316 out of 161,956, including artillery), 12 per cent in 1809, and 11.3 per cent by September 1813 (29,504 cavalry out of 260,797). When the militia is included as part of the force permanently under arms, the percentage of cavalry was reduced further, for example to 8 per cent in 1805 and 9 per cent in September 1813. From 1807 the number of cavalry remained fairly constant, between 26,000 and 29,000.

At the time, the cavalry tended to be somewhat discounted by the remainder of the army; for example, George Gleig of the 85th Light Infantry

Light dragoons, in the uniform worn up to 1812, showing the dress shabraque and hussar bridle. (Print after Harry Payne, a non-contemporary image)

wrote of the infantry and cavalry, 'the former ... regarding the latter as more ornamental than useful, the latter regarding the former as extremely ungenteel'. A similar opinion was overheard by Francis Skelly Tidy among the 14th Foot at Waterloo, when one man remarked, 'They have driven back the Hussars!' 'What of that?' replied his neighbour. 'They must blow off the froth before they get to the porter.' In fact, however, the cavalry formed an integral part of the army, performing duties vital to the success of the other 'arms'; as the Foot Guards were heard to shout to the 7th and 15th Light Dragoons on their going into action at Mouveaux on 17 May 1794, 'if you lather, we'll shave them!'

RECRUITMENT & CONDITIONS

The rank and file of the cavalry were recruited, as for the rest of the army, by voluntary enlistment. A recruiting poster of the 14th Light Dragoons described some of those most likely to enlist: 'All you who are kicking your heels behind a solitary desk with too little wages, and a pinch-gut Master – all you with too much wife, or are perplexed with obstinate and unfeeling parents.' Although the appeal was principally to the unemployed or those tired of the impecunious grind of civilian labour, it is easy to overemphasise the duplicity of recruiters who enticed the naïve into enlisting, and the criminal element among the recruits; Wellington's often misquoted remark concerning 'the scum of the earth' was made in relation to the need to widen the social background of recruits, and his addition that 'it is really wonderful that we should have made them the fine fellows they are' is a more accurate reflection.

It is difficult to provide a truly comprehensive analysis of the nature of those who enrolled in the army. Recruits had to be physically fit, swearing upon oath that they did not suffer from fits nor were ruptured; such was the severity of manual labour that it was estimated that one-eighth of the labouring population had a rupture. In 1806 height restrictions were 5 feet 4 inches for general service and an inch more for those choosing their own regiments. It was generally a little more for foot guards and cavalry while some restrictions were imposed for certain regiments: in August 1812, for example, it was reported that the 10th Hussars intended to discharge all men under 5 feet 7 inches. In the period just after the Napoleonic Wars, an analysis of 1,000 men accepted as fit showed that 549 were under 5 feet 7 inches, and only 49 over 5 feet 10 inches; the average chest measurement was only 32.6 inches, 'country recruits' being on average $\frac{3}{4}$ in. larger than those from towns.

Most recruits were young; it was stated in 1839 that those who enlisted at the age of 25 or more were 'habitually dissipated and profligate characters, broken-down gentlemen, discharged soldiers, deserters, &c.', and that perhaps a few as five per cent were still fit for service at the age of 40. As many as two-thirds were unable to sign their own name, though literacy was markedly greater among Scottish recruits. An analysis of the 1811 census showed that in England 35 per cent of the population was employed in agriculture, 45 per cent in trade, manufacture or

A recruiting-party of light dragoons enlists a countryman, who tries on a helmet and sabre to the despair of his family. Note the Negro trumpeter: exotically dressed musicians were an aid to recruiting. (Mezzotint by C. Turner after John Eckstein, 1803)

A trooper of the 4th Dragoon Guards, showing the continuing use of the basket hilted 1788-style sabre. (Print from the British Military Library, 1799)

each of the following occupations: silversmith, stay-maker, cutler, sawyer, spur-maker, collier, wheelwright, cloth-maker, tailor, spinner and even a sailor (the latter an escaped Negro slave from North Carolina).

To those living in poverty, the bounty paid to each recruit upon enlistment was a major attraction: it rose from £7/12/6d. in 1803 to £23/17/6d. in 1812 for those enlisting for life, and five guineas less for a seven-year enlistment. The latter, 'limited service' enlistment, was introduced in 1806; for the cavalry the initial period was for ten years, with two possible extensions of seven years each. The bounty was often an illusory boon, as recruits discovered that some was withheld to pay for part of their kit, and the rest was often drunk by the recruiting-party, whom the recruit was expected to treat. An 11th Light Dragoon writing in the *United Service Journal* in 1840 described how predatory NCOs would give favoured treatment only until the money was gone: 'They will first suck you dry, and then grind you to powder'; and in July 1809 a recruit in the 18th Light Dragoons who refused to squander his bounty on his fellows was tossed in a blanket, and died from a broken neck when one corner accidentally gave way.

The vast majority enlisted for life, their service terminated only by death, incapacitating injury or disease, or discharge when their services were no longer required. Thus, a man might spend virtually his entire adult life in the one regiment: for example, at their deaths in 1800 and 1811 respectively, quartermasters Thomas Page of the 4th Dragoons and Barnes of the Royal Horse Guards had each spent fifty years in their respective regiments. Some men enlisted from a desire for glory or a glamorous uniform, illusions which were generally dispelled rapidly. This reason and lack of funds probably led the poet Coleridge to enlist in the 15th Light Dragoons in 1793, under the alias of Silas Tomkyn Comberbatch; he soon realised the wretchedness of his condition and his brother, a captain, arranged for his discharge!

The officers

Although cavalry officers occupied a somewhat privileged position, especially in fashionable regiments like the 10th Hussars, they obtained their commissions in the same way as the remainder of the

handicraft, and 20 per cent lived on the rental of property or on interest from capital; in Wales agricultural workers outnumbered the manufacturers by two to one. The occupations of recruits varied with the areas from which they were drawn and with any depressions in particular trades, and although the cavalry was regarded as superior to the infantry, few recruits can have had much experience of managing horses. A random sample of 50 recruits whose occupations are recorded reveals a selection of trades much the same as for typical infantry recruits, with only four having the chance of previous experience with horses: a farrier, a waggoner, a farm servant and a farm labourer. The remainder of the sample included 15 weavers, 14 labourers, two framework knitters, two calico printers, two hosiers, and one

Table A: Purchasing a commission

Rank	Life Guards	Royal Horse Guards	Cavalry	Infantry
Lt. Colonel	£5,200	£4,950	£4,982/10/-	£3,500
Major	£4,250	£4,050	£3,882/10/-	£2,600
Captain	£3,100	£2,950	£2,782/10/-	£1,500
Lieutenant	£1,750	£1,350	£997/10/-	£550
Cornet/Ensign	£1,600	£1,050	£735	£400

army. Any young man might apply if he could provide a recommendation and afford to purchase his rank, which led to the unsatisfactory practice of commissioning children; before the system was reformed in 1802 some 20 per cent of new officers were under 15 years of age. After 1802 a minimum age of 16 was specified, but even after that half the new appointments were under the age of 20. Promotion was partly by seniority and partly by purchase, and not until 1809 was the system regulated to prevent incompetents buying their way immediately to high command. The purchase system has been overstated, however, and by the time of the Peninsular War it accounted for less than one-fifth of promotions, and for all its ills did permit those of genuine talent to rise to positions of responsibility at an early age. The price charged for cavalry commissions meant that cavalry officers needed a degree of financial independence greater than that of the infantry; the rates can be seen in Table A.

Officers' pay was claimed to be less than it had been in 1695, once taxes were deducted, and although cavalry pay was greater than that of the infantry, cavalry officers required a private income even to pay for their kit. The daily pay, compared to that of the infantry, can be seen in Table B.

Officers' pensions were much more generous than those granted to the other ranks: those whose services were not required might be granted permanent half-pay for their rank, and for every lost eye or limb a colonel would receive £300 p.a., a major £200, a captain £100, a lieutenant £70, and a cornet £50.

Contrary to popular belief, the majority of cavalry officers were not members of the aristocracy but from the country gentry or professional classes. For example, of 329 troop officers at Waterloo (i.e. excluding staff and administrative officers, and including one volunteer from the Ceylon Regt.), there was only one peer (the Earl of Portarlington, 23rd

Table B: Daily pay for officers

Rank	Life Guards	Cavalry	Infantry
Colonel	36/-	32/10d.	22/6d.
Lt. Colonel	31/-	23/-	15/11d.
Major	26/-	19/3d.	14/1d.
Captain	16/-	14/7d.	9/5d.
Lieutenant	11/-	9/-	5/8d.
Cornet/Ensign	8/6d.	8/-	4/8d.
Quartermaster	6/-	5/6d.	5/8d.
Surgeon	12/-	12/-	9/5d.

Light Dragoons), 13 sons of peers, 17 sons of baronets, two knights, one son of a knight, one Italian prince (Paul Ruffo, Prince Castelcicala, 6th Dragoons), one Hanoverian baron (Wilhelm Osten, 16th Light Dragoons) and one son of a German (Berg) countess (Henry Acton, 18th Light Dragoons, whose father was a general in the Neapolitan army).

Though uncommon, it was possible for a man to rise to high rank from humble background, as exemplified by two officers at Waterloo. Sir John Elley of the Royal Horse Guards was the son of an eating-house keeper and apprenticed to a tanner, who enlisted in the regiment as a private and ended his career as a lieutenant-general; James Inglis Hamilton, lieutenant-colonel of the 2nd Dragoons (killed at Waterloo), was the son of Sgt. Maj. William Anderson of the 21st Foot, born on campaign in America in 1777 and who rose through the commissioned ranks by the patronage of his father's old commanding officer, whose name he took.

The appointment of regimental colonel was almost always bestowed upon a general officer for long or distinguished service (in the cavalry, only the Prince of Wales, colonel of the 10th Light Dragoons 1796–1820, was not a professional officer). The appointment was often for life, although a colonel might relinquish it to take up a similar position in another regiment. Throughout the period, only one cavalry colonel gave up his position for any other reason: Hugh Percy, 2nd Duke of Northumberland, who resigned the colonelcy of the Royal Horse Guards in 1806 when the Duke of York denied his request for the unprecedented power to appoint and promote the regiment's officers. During the period of the French Revolutionary and Napoleonic Wars, the 2nd Dragoons had the most colonels of any regiment, six; conversely, five regiments had a single colonel throughout, the 1st Life Guards, 5th and 6th Dragoon Guards, and 16th and 18th Light Dragoons. Charles Moore, 1st Marquess of Drogheda, was colonel of the 18th for 62 years (1759–1821), including the first three years as lieutenant-colonel-commandant; he raised the regiment in 1759 and outlived it, as it was disbanded in the year of his death (22 December 1821, at the age of 91). A regimental colonelcy was a ceremonial and administrative appointment; colonels did not command their regiments on active service, but received a salary and were responsible for the clothing of the regiment, from the purchase of which it was possible to make a

An officer of the 10th Light Dragoons, showing the 1796 light cavalry uniform; note the clipped tail of the *horse. (Print from the British Military Library, 1799)*

Table C: Daily pay for Other Ranks

Rank	Life Guards	Cavalry	Infantry
Sergeant	—	2/2d.	1/10¾d.
Corporal	2/6¼d.	1/7½d.	1/2¼d.
Private	1/11¼d.	1/3d.	1/-
Trumpeter/ Drummer	2/6d.	1/7d.	1/1¼d.

(In the Life Guards, sergeants were styled 'corporals')

considerable profit (many colonels did not, but in November 1798 the *Morning Chronicle* claimed that the colonel of an infantry battalion could make between £400 and £800 per annum on its uniforms!).

Various deductions were made from this pay, for example 4d. per week for laundry. The daily subsistence allowance for a horse (9d., 1/3d. in the Life Guards) was made in addition to the above, hence alternative statistics which give the daily pay of a cavalry private as 2/-, etc. Royal Horse Guards' pay was between that of the Life Guards and the ordinary cavalry: for a corporal 2/3¼d., for a private 1/8¼d., for example, plus the horse allowance. On the march the soldier received 9d., which with 6d. from his pay and 1d. beer-money went to the innkeeper upon whom he was billeted, in return for lodging and three meals. In quarters, when food was supplied by the government, 2d. per day was paid to the innkeeper to cover bed, five pints of small beer or cider, salt, vinegar and cooking utensils, though if the commanding officer were agreeable, the 2d. could be paid to the soldier to make his own lodging arrangements. In barracks there was no cash allowance, but bed, coal, candles, cooking utensils and five pints of small beer were allowed per day. In camp there was no beer ration, but instead bread was available at reduced prices, plus a cash allowance of ¾d. per day.

The official daily ration consisted of 1½ lbs. of flour or bread, 1 lb. of beef or ½ lb. of pork, ¼ pint of peas, 1 oz. of butter or cheese and 1 oz. of rice. Variations were permitted, and when the 'small species' were not available on campaign (i.e. everything save bread and meat), the daily ration was 1½ lbs. of flour or bread and 1½ lbs. of beef or 10 oz. of pork. All cooking was done by the soldiers themselves, in small 'messes'. Regimental baggage-waggons were not generally used to transport rations, this being the responsibility of the commissariat department. Although Wellington in particular took great care to ensure continuity of supply, at times on campaign this proved impossible, and several accounts describe how men might be reduced to eating acorns or even leaves until rations finally arrived.

Home service

For regiments serving at home, increasing use was made of barracks built specifically for cavalry, which included not only stabling and forage stores but in the larger ones riding schools, veterinary hospitals and blacksmith's and saddler's shops. A barracks at Kensington may have existed as early as 1702, but in the 18th century it was thought that billeting men among the civilian population was preferable, and that barrack-building was unconstitutional. Fox and Grey supported a resolution before parliament in 1793 which associated barracks with military repression, but Pitt countered the argument by stating that barracks would prevent friction between soldiers and civilians, and would separate the troops from the seditious sentiments held by some members of the population.

By July 1794 seven cavalry barracks were in occupation, at Birmingham, Coventry, Hounslow, Manchester, Norwich, Nottingham and Sheffield; the largest, Manchester, could house only 324 men, Norwich 216, Hounslow 270 and the others 162 men each. Eighteen more were building and a further 23 were planned; 25 of these were to accommodate only a single troop. Others were added in later years, at considerable expense: Weymouth cavalry barracks, for example, ready in August 1798, cost £59,089/11/-; Brighton (completed June 1795) £49,574/9s./8d.; and Eastbourne (1800–02) only £5,216/18s./11d. Objections continued, however, and after the Life Guards had been evicted from their rented London barracks in King St. (which were re-let for a short term at exorbitant cost) the proposal to build a new one, and also barracks at Liverpool and Bristol and new stables at Brighton, provoked a furious row in parliament in spring 1812. The opposition MP Samuel Whitbread asked if barracks were to be 'fortresses for controlling the citizens', and Sir Francis Burdett stated that 'the object of Govern-

William Warre of the 16th Light Dragoons (later of the Portuguese staff), showing the use of an item of hussar uniform (the pelisse) by an ordinary light dragoon regiment. (Print after J.C.D. Engleheart)

ment in erecting barracks all over the country was, that they might use the troops paid by the people to subdue the people'. Nevertheless, the construction of these barracks was subsequently approved by parliament.

Discipline

Discipline was draconian, the commonest form of punishment being flogging with a cat o' nine tails on the bare back. Up to 1,200 lashes could be awarded; sentences of 1,000 were not uncommon, and 3–700 commonplace, yet even those who suffered in this way generally thought it necessary to control the hard core of 'incorrigibles' which existed in every regiment.

It was often stated that most punishments occurred in regiments with the worst commanders; speaking on this subject in the House of Commons in June 1811, the radical M.P. Sir Francis Burdett quoted the example of Ernest, Duke of Cumberland.

9

The king's fifth son, the duke was an experienced officer but one of sinister aspect (he was popularly, if wrongly, believed to have raped his sister and murdered his valet), and was given command in 1801 of the 15th Light Dragoons, a regiment 'long distinguished for its efficiency in the field, and for its peaceable, modest and proper demeanour', according to Burdett, who claimed that within a very few months more 'cruel punishments' took place in the regiment than had been necessary in the entire period from the Seven Years' War to Cumberland's assumption of command.

A similar commanding officer was George Quentin of the 10th Hussars, who between December 1812 and July 1814 (most of the time on campaign) awarded no less than 34,300 lashes, of which 21,895

were actually administered, ranging from 600 for plundering to 20 (out of 200 ordered) for being absent without leave, and 50 for killing a fowl. Out of 134 cases, 66 were the direct result of drunkenness, including 41 of being drunk on duty.

Apart from promotion, there existed no official system of awards or medals to reward brave or deserving soldiers; indeed, when the newspaper *The Independent Whig* raised this matter, its proprietor was tried for libel on the grounds that even to mention such a thing was intended to excite disaffection in the army! (He was acquitted when it was proved that at the time of publication he was in Dorchester Gaol, and thus had no control over what his newspaper printed!) Some regiments awarded medals privately to deserving soldiers, and such

A dragoon trooper wearing the 1812 uniform, with the dress breeches and long boots, and showing the heavy cavalry bridle. (Print after Harry Payne)

awards may have been accompanied by preferential treatment: for example, Levi Grisdale, a hero of the 10th Hussars who had captured General Lefebvre-Desnouëttes at Benevente, was convicted in February 1813 of being drunk and absent from barracks; but even under the harsh rule then in force in the regiment, he was neither reduced to the ranks nor flogged, but merely given a temporary suspension of rank, a singular sentence in the regiment's punishment-lists.

Soldiers incapacitated by wounds or disease on service could apply for a pension from the hospitals of Chelsea or Kilmainham (near Dublin). Blindness or the loss of a limb warranted a pension of 1/6d. per diem for sergeants, 1/2d. for corporals and 1/- for privates, and Chelsea Hospital out-pensioners could be granted pensions ranging from £18/5/- per annum (1st class) to £13/13/- (2nd) and £7/12/- (3rd). Those having lost more than one limb or eye, or who were otherwise totally incapacitated, could receive up to 3/6d. (sergeant), 3/- (corporal), and 2/6d. (private) per diem. These sums were not generous: in the immediate post-Waterloo period, for example, when the average army pension was 9/11d. per week (almost a quarter being only 3/6d. per week), a cotton-spinner could earn 24/- per week.

The brutal aspects of military service, the fact that most soldiers were drawn from the lowest classes of society, and the use of troops in police actions 'in support of civil power', gave the military a poor reputation among much of the civilian population, so that, as one veteran admitted, 'whoever " 'listed for a soldier" was at once set down among a catalogue of persons who had turned out ill'. Relations between civilians and military, especially when the latter were used in the absence of any organised police, were thus often uneasy, and violent outbreaks occurred throughout the period. In July 1795, for example, two 12th Light Dragoons attempting to arrest a deserter in Holborn were attacked by the crowd and severely beaten, and rescued only with difficulty after one of the soldiers in defending himself had cut off the nose of one of the mob, which, the *London Chronicle* reported, served only to 'irritate' him further! Nevertheless, despite the hardships of an often brutal existence and the often poor reputation of the military trade, rarely does there appear to have been a shortage of recruits.

The proportions and somewhat impractical nature of the hussar busby are illustrated in this portrait of Edward Kerrison of the 7th Hussars, in the uniform of a general officer of hussars. (Print after M.A. Shee)

In Cossall churchyard, Nottinghamshire, is a monument to three ordinary cavalrymen whose motivations for enlistment seem to exemplify the reasons why men forsook the safety of civilian life. John Shaw fell out with his master, abandoned his apprenticeship, and joined the 2nd Life Guards to advance his career as a boxer (which prospered in the Household Cavalry). Richard Waplington joined the same regiment to escape the coal-mines in which he had worked from the age of 12 or 13; and Thomas Wheatley fled to the 23rd Light Dragoons after trying to shoot his father who was breaking the strike of stocking-weavers which Thomas supported. Wheatley survived to return home and is buried beneath the monument; Shaw and Waplington lie in unmarked graves at Waterloo.

TRAINING

Training was generally carried out at regimental depots, and there were also central establishments like the Cavalry Depot at Maidstone. Although the Earl of Pembroke (colonel of the 1st Dragoons 1764–94) had published his book *Military Equitation* as early as 1761, even as late as 1773 only the Royal Horse Guards and 2nd Dragoon Guards had purpose-built riding schools. Training of riding was not standardised, but was undertaken by each regiment's riding-master and 'rough riders' (at least one corporal per troop, who were excused guard and stable duty). The riding-master was also responsible for the schooling of horses and supervision of the rough riders, whom he had to teach (according to the 1814 *Standing Orders* of the 1st Life Guards) to 'give the words of command with spirit', in a manner 'cool and temperate, and to refrain from swearing, or using improper language, and from harshness to either man or horse'.

A system of universal training was attempted in India by General Sir John Floyd (who had fought as a cornet at Emsdorf at the age of 12!), and who in 1808 instructed one officer and one rough rider from each regiment in his own method of equitation. A central cavalry depot, modelled on that at Maidstone, was established at Arcot under Sir Rollo Gillespie in April 1807, but it did not find favour with the military establishment and it was abolished in February 1808. Such attempts were not without effect, however: Capt. Lawrence Neville of Floyd's regiment (19th Light Dragoons) wrote an instruction manual which was still in use in India in 1827, and in 1811 the publication of *A Riding Lesson, suggested by Lieutenant General Floyd* was the foundation of the improved riding school system.

Heavy cavalry normally rode with long stirrups and extended legs, but the light cavalry was instructed to adjust its stirrups so that when the rider stood up there would be four inches between seat and saddle, a style coming into use with civilians for hunting or riding at speed. In his *Cavalry Equitation* (1797), Lt. Col. Tyndale of the 1st Life Guards condemned the 'long' seat as commonly taught by military riding-masters, and recommended the 'shorter' seat as enabling the rider to sit more securely, and as permitting him to support his back against his valise when sleeping in the saddle on the march. To provide extra security, stirrups were sometimes shortened before combat, as happened at Laswaree.

Whether from imperfect schooling of horses or training, the standard of horsemanship was in some cases not high, and many injuries were caused by falls in unexpected circumstances. These even occurred on ceremonial occasions: in November 1809 when escorting the King from Windsor to London, a Royal Horse Guard was 'very much hurt' when thrown from an ill-trained horse which had hospitalised its previous rider, and another member of the escort was so out of control that the horse ran off and bowled

A private of the Cavalry Staff Corps, a provost unit formed in 1813 also as couriers and orderlies; the uniform is in the 1812 light dragoon style, but in red with blue facings and white lace. The inscription on the valise, 'SD/A', indicates 'Staff Dragoons, troop A'. (Aquatint by I.C. Stadler after Charles Hamilton Smith, from the latter's Costume of the Army of the British Empire, *published May 1813)*

over one of the King's mounted attendants. Even officers, most of whom would have ridden from childhood, suffered many accidents: in 1806 the 6th Dragoon Guards even lost their lieutenant-colonel (Bagwell) who was killed on the spot by a horse which ran away with him. A trooper of the 23rd Light Dragoons recalled that on landing in Portugal, the horses were so young and skittish that it was almost impossible to manage them; he was thrown six times in the first march, and only solved the problem by adjusting the harness of his 'beast, that all his pranks were insufficient . . . to incommode me in my seat'.

Tactical training was determined initially at regimental level; for example, in 1786 it was reported that the commanding officer of the 8th Light Dragoons had introduced what he called a war whoop, which was described as being the cause of great confusion! A standard system of manoeuvre was introduced in 1795, and a standard sword-exercise and set of trumpet calls in the following year, but these were not directed primarily towards the requirements of active service; the prescribed manoeuvres were condemned by Ludlow Beamish of the King's German Legion as efforts 'which, like Chinese puzzles, only engross time and labour to the unprofitable end of forming useless combinations'. Even relatively simple manoeuvres were made complex; for example, when a regiment in line changed its facing by pivoting on the central squadron, some 35 verbal commands were required. The official *Instruc-*

One of the best units in the army, the 3rd Hussars of the King's German Legion, is depicted here with the line and light infantry of the Legion. (Aquatint by I.C. Stadler after Charles Hamilton Smith, published April 1815)

tions and Regulations for the Formations and Movements of the Cavalry confirmed the squadron and troop as the principal manoeuvre elements, though sub-units included half-squadrons (two equal parts, not necessarily each an independent troop), divisions (quarter-squadron) and sub-divisions (eighth-squadron); manoeuvre was mostly in threes.

Part of the reason for lack of control in action, which so bedevilled British cavalry, was the sacrifice of order for speed in training. William Tomkinson of the 16th Light Dragoons condemned the practice of 'each regiment estimating its merit by the celerity of movement ... we do everything so quickly that it is impossible men can understand what they are about ... Before the enemy, excepting in charging, I never saw troops go beyond a trot ... In England I never saw nor heard of cavalry taught to charge, disperse, and form, which, if I only taught a regiment one thing, I think it should be that'. Yet, commenting on the sortie made by the 15th Light Dragoons from Nijmegen in November 1794, *The British Military Journal* noted that although their commanding general, 'a foreigner, was exasperated at the quickness and irregularity of the charge', it advised that 'when infantry are flying in all directions', for cavalry to operate with 'form or exactness' (other than the maintenance of a reserve) 'may lose them the opportunity of doing material mischief to their enemies', as good as sanctioning the uncontrolled charge.

Heavy and light cavalry in the 1812 uniforms, attired for bad weather in cloaks and head-dress with waterproof covers.

(Aquatint by I.C. Stadler after Charles Hamilton Smith, published June 1815)

Accounts of manoeuvres prove the validity of Tomkinson's complaints, such as the *Morning Chronicle*'s description of the 10th Light Dragoons' field-day on Wimbledon Common in July 1798, performed over ground so slippery and presumably at such a pace that four riders fell and were injured. The same journal carried a telling account of training at Swinley near Windsor in the following August, involving 'six veteran regiments, every one of which had served three campaigns on the Continent' and Sir David Dundas, known as 'Old Pivot' from his authorship of the infantry drill-manual:

'The rapidity with which the men were led over the ground, bad enough to appal the boldest fox-hunter, occasioned several officers to predict the breaking of some of their necks. No fatal accident, however, happened till the 27th of August, when a private of the 7th Light Dragoons fell, with his horse, and died the next day. On the other days five or six falls generally occurred, but the mischief was confined to the destruction of horses, broken bones and bruises ... nobody showed a greater alacrity in falling off than General David Dundas. He was once overturned in a buggy, and twice he fell from his horse in the middle of the field, and in the presence of his Majesty. The complete revolutions he made in his way from the saddle to the ground entitle him to the praise of an excellent tumbler, and give him new claims to the sobriquet of Pivot Dundas ... The six Regiments of which the Camp was composed, are confessedly the elite of the British Cavalry ... A defect, however, with which our horse is often reproached by foreigners still exists. They are not well broke to fire. When *feux de joye* were fired on the birth days of the Prince of Wales and Duke of York, a great number of horses were so scared by the report of the pistols, as to run out of the ranks, in spite of all the efforts of their riders'.

Even on campaign the training undertaken was not always appreciated nor beneficial: when Stapleton Cotton held a field day of two brigades in 1812, Wellington rode off half-way through, saying of his cavalry commander, 'What the devil is he about now?'!

TACTICS

The cavalry's reputation was exemplified by Wellington's comment that 'I considered our cavalry so inferior to the French for want of order, that although I considered one of our squadrons a match for two French, yet I did not care to see four British opposed to four French, and still more so as the numbers increased, and order (of course) became more necessary. They could gallop, but could not preserve their order'. After a charge at Maguilla (11 June 1812) had enjoyed initial success, then raced on and been routed, Wellington stormed: 'It is occasioned entirely by the trick our officers of cavalry have acquired of galloping at every thing, and their galloping back as fast as they gallop on the enemy. They never consider their situation, and never think of manoeuvring before an enemy – so little that one would think they cannot manoeuvre, excepting on Wimbledon Common; and when they use their arm as it ought to be used, viz., offensively, they never keep nor provide for a reserve. All cavalry should charge in two lines, of which one should be in reserve; if obliged to charge in one line, part of the line, at least one-third, should be ordered beforehand to pull up, and form in second line, as soon as the charge should be given, and the enemy has been broken and has retired.'

The *Instructions and Regulations* did stress the importance of maintaining order and rallying after the first shock of a charge, but emphasised 'the greatest velocity ... possible' and that 'the spur as much as the sword tends to overset an opposite enemy'. The mechanics of the charge were specified: to begin at a walk, with the sword-blade resting on the right arm; then increase to a brisk trot until within 250 yards of the enemy, with the sword-hand steadied on the right thigh and the point of the sword inclined slightly forwards; then gallop, with the sword in the same position; and 80 yards from the enemy, upon the order 'charge', the gallop increased to the fastest speed possible and the sword-arm lifted,

the sword pointed towards the enemy and carried crossways to the head.

Attacks were normally executed in two ranks and in line, but individual squadrons or troops could operate independently within the concept of the line. A writer in the *British Military Journal* (1799) stated that attacks were normally conducted in echelon of squadrons, those in the rear following at 150-yard intervals, the leading squadron attracting the enemy's fire and those following then falling upon the enemy before they had had time to reload. Succeeding squadrons would alter course slightly to strike the enemy a little way to one side or the other of the breach in the enemy line made by the first squadron. Three or four ranks' depth was recommended against

Capt. Alexander Sinclair Gordon of the London and Westminster Light Horse Volunteers, c. 1796, showing typical light dragoon uniform and an exotic leopardskin shabraque; the regiment wore scarlet jackets with black facings and silver lace. (Engraving by A. Carden after A.W. Devis)

Horse furniture at its most basic is illustrated in this print of the Surrey Yeomanry, a corps which wore light blue jackets with scarlet facings and silver lace; note the white head-collar in addition to the leather bridle. (Aquatint by and after Charles Tomkins, 1800)

enemy cavalry, where there would be no musketry to disorder the attack (when a fallen horse could bring down all those behind it), but it was also thought that depth should be sacrificed to ensure that the line was no shorter than that of the enemy, thus leaving no exposed flank. Against infantry in square, attacks were advised to be made simultaneously against a face and at least one corner, in waves 150 yards apart, with thirty-yard gaps in the second and succeeding waves to allow the first to retire without disordering those following.

When skirmishers were deployed, they were ordered to precede the main body by at least 200 yards and to operate in two lines, the first to fire and then withdraw through the rear line or, when advancing, to stand fast while the rear line advanced to the front. Officers and sergeants were positioned between the two lines. Skirmishers were ordered to fire on horseback and to their left, the most convenient direction when the butt was at the right shoulder. When skirmishing with pistols instead of carbines, the sword was to be suspended by its knot from the wrist, ready for immediate use.

Inadequate training was not the only reason why troops so often failed to rally after a charge, causing such dire consequences. Although most officers performed their duties assiduously, there were a number of noted incompetents, although few were as useless as the most famous of them, the Prince of Wales's crony George 'Beau' Brummel. He served in the Prince's regiment (10th Light Dragoons) 1795–98 and was so neglectful of his duty that it was said he was unable to recognise his own troop, and resigned his captaincy when the regiment was ordered to Manchester, reputedly declaring that he was unwilling to go on foreign service! Another officer from this regiment, though later a brave and resourceful man, was so inveterate a gambler that he received permanent leave of absence to prevent his habits rubbing off on his fellows. The commander of the 1st Life Guards, Major Camac, who joined the Peninsular army in 1812 was unable to perform a simple manoeuvre when requested by his general, and was told in public to report to his own adjutant to be taught what to do. In a fit of pique he then attempted to manoeuvre his regiment, rode them into the sea in error and almost drowned the man at the end of the line.

Another commanding officer of dubious worth was George Quentin of the 10th Hussars, who was court-martialled after a revolt by almost all his officers. A friend of the Prince of Wales and originally a member of the Hanoverian army, Quentin was exonerated and all his accusers were transferred from the regiment, yet the evidence given was convincing. Lack of decisive command was evident at Toulouse, when Quentin disappeared and left his leading squadrons without orders and under fire. In this situation the lower ranks showed similar indecision, the senior officer present, Maj. Howard, asking his subordinate, Capt. Fitzclarence, 'what shall we do now?'! Despite a number of contemporary accounts of conflict and even hooliganism among the ranks of regimental officers, however, such people were in a very small minority.

Another factor which probably had a marked effect was the inexperience of regiments: in a number of the least successful actions, the troops involved were either newly arrived on campaign or executing their first charge; only after a period of active service did they become as proficient as they should have been had domestic training been adequate.

After further examples of charges getting out of hand and undoing their original success, Wellington was compelled to issue detailed instructions after Waterloo concerning the correct method of executing a charge, which provides the best guide to handling cavalry in action. First, a reserve should be kept to second a successful charge or cover a retreat, never less than half the total strength, and up to two-thirds. Cavalry should deploy in three bodies, the first two in line and the third in column, but able to deploy rapidly. The second line should be 400–500 yards behind the first, and the reserve a similar distance

Light dragoons on the march, receiving refreshments at an inn; their head-dress are the cylindrical 'watering caps'. (Print after J.A. Atkinson)

behind the second, this space being sufficient for a defeated first line to retire without disordering the second, but sufficiently close for the supports to be able effectively to assist the first line. Against infantry, the second line should be 200 yards behind the first, thus able to second the charge of the first line before the enemy could reload. When the first line charged, the supports should follow at a walk, and on no account become carried away with enthusiasm so as to lose formation or cohesion.

The necessity of maintaining a reserve was as important as the need to rally after the first shock, especially as a guard against counter-attack; indeed, in some of the most successful cavalry actions it was notable that there was no enemy reserve available immediately to exploit any British disorganization.

Scouting and skirmishing

Scouting and skirmishing had to be learned entirely on campaign, despite the efforts of a few officers who had urged the training of such tactics at home as early as the 1790s. Among these was General Money, who had served in the French army until Britain entered the war, who published pamphlets in favour of training light cavalry in skirmish tactics and dismounted fighting like the French chasseurs, initially

Left: Skirmishing on horseback: a trooper of the 15th Hussars loading his carbine while the weapon is still attached to the swivel on his belt. (Aquatint by I.C. Stadler after Charles Hamilton Smith, published September 1812)

Right: Henry William Paget, Earl of Uxbridge and later 1st Marquess of Anglesey, perhaps the most famous of the cavalry commanders of the period, in the uniform of his 7th Light Dragoons (Hussars). (Print after Henry Edridge, 1808)

to oppose the threatened invasion of Britain where, he stated, the progress of enclosure was so widespread that a regiment could not form in line anywhere and be out of range of hedgerows behind which infantry could shelter.

Nevertheless, 'outpost' training was neglected totally, as described by William Tomkinson of the 16th Light Dragoons: 'To attempt giving men or officers any idea in England of outpost duty was considered absurd, and when they came abroad, they had all this to learn. The fact was, there was no one to teach them. Sir Stapleton Cotton tried, at Woodbridge in Suffolk, with the 14th and 16th Light

Dragoons, and got the enemy's vedettes and his own looking the same way.' There was not even any universal system of signalling. The 16th Light Dragoons in the Peninsula in 1810 evolved the following: upon the appearance of the enemy, the sentry raised his helmet on his carbine, circling his horse to the left to signal the approach of cavalry, to the right for infantry. If the enemy advanced rapidly he cantered in a circle, and if not noticed fired his carbine. He held his post until the enemy was near, then retired, repeatedly firing his carbine.

The Hussars of the King's German Legion were acknowledged as the 'outpost' experts par excellence, probably because of their experienced German officers. The assiduous way in which they undertook their duties is exemplified by the story concerning an officer at the end of the Peninsular War, when hostilities had ended. Being seen preparing to sleep in full equipment, he was asked, 'You surely don't mean to sleep in your clothes tonight, when you know there is an armistice?' 'Air mistress or no air mistress,' replied the hussar, 'I sleeps in my breeches!'

It took some experience of campaigning for British regiments to become equally proficient. That they did is demonstrated by the exploit at Blascho Sancho, three days after the Battle of Salamanca, when Cpl. William Hanley of the 14th Light Dragoons led a patrol of four of his regiment and four of the 1st K.G.L. Hussars, reconnoitring in advance of his brigade. His force was reduced by one when Pvt. Luke Billingham accidentally shot his horse in the shoulder when checking his pistol. Learning from Spanish civilians of the presence of French troops some two leagues away at Blascho Sancho, Hanley sent out several scouts in advance and marched towards the village. He watched from a hill until a column of French infantry had marched away, then led his patrol into the village, capturing four enemy dragoons who were cutting forage, and making for a house with a walled stable-yard. This building housed an enemy troop; having captured its officer who had attempted to shoot him through the front window, Hanley ordered his men to fire through the single door of the courtyard to keep the inhabitants pinned down. Using one of the K.G.L. hussars as an interpreter, Hanley threatened to burn the building around their ears; whereupon a sergeant and 26 dragoons filed out, surrendering their weapons which

Hanley's men smashed. Hanley formed his prisoners into a four-deep column and was about to move off when a French colonel rode up and seeing so few British soldiers presumed them to be the prisoners; he patted Hanley's shoulder and said, 'Bonjour Englishman', whereupon Hanley presented his pistol at the colonel's breast. Adding the colonel and his servant to the column, Hanley set off at a fast pace, marching through the night in 'what cheered us most, a beautifully bright moonlight'. Hanley eventually reached his own regiment's camp, alarming the sentries by the sight of so many long-tailed horses (i.e. not British), and being greeted by the cheers of the whole camp. The exploit was mentioned in official despatches (almost unprecedentedly, given that no officer was involved), the patrol received not only the usual bounty of £25 per captured horse, but on Wellington's instruction each man received a further 12 dollars; and Hanley received 24 dollars and a regimental medal. After 34 years' service he retired from the 14th Light Dragoons as a sergeant-major.

REGIMENTAL ORGANISATION

Cavalry regiments were divided into heavy and light, the former in theory best suited for 'shock' action and the latter also adept at 'outpost' duty, skirmishing and reconnaissance; but in many cases the difference was not marked. Indeed, a writer in the *United Service Journal* in 1834 considered it futile to make any distinction: 'cavalry, to be light or strong, must be mounted on horses fully equal to the weight they have to carry ... heavy cavalry and heavy infantry are terms for heavy heads to amuse themselves with; in modern war, cavalry and infantry, if they are to be strong, must be light also'. There was no difference

Left: Watering horses, showing a trooper in stable dress with a common style of flat, soft cloth forage cap. (Print published by S. & J. Fuller)

Below: Exercising horses, with troopers in stable dress. (Print published by S. & J. Fuller)

between the seven regiments of Dragoon Guards and the six (later five) of Dragoons, the differing titles resulting simply from the conversion of the original Regiments of Horse to Dragoon Guards in 1746. The Light Dragoons were numbered consecutively after the 6th Dragoons, the number rising (albeit briefly) to 33.

From April 1799 there was a vacant number in the list, caused by the disbandment of the 5th Dragoons, an unfortunate corps which had spent about half a century in Ireland. This followed a plot among some members to rebel and murder their officers and the loyal members of the regiment, the malcontents being newly enrolled Irish rebels apparently led by one James M'Nassar, a notorious bad character who turned informer and implicated two other dragoons, the Feney brothers. It was stated at the time that 'almost every regiment belonging to the Irish establishment, was more or less tainted by the admission of disaffected persons', and despite the previous good service of the regiment and the small number of men involved, it was resolved 'to make this severe example' by disbanding the regiment.

This was an isolated incident: throughout the period the army remained steadfastly non-political, and although in the early 1790s copies of Paine's *Rights of Man* circulated in soldiers' hands, they had little effect. A political club in the 2nd Dragoons was suppressed in 1792, but even that seems to have been concerned mainly with improving the pay.

The 7th, 10th, 15th and 18th Light Dragoons were converted to Hussars in 1806–07, which involved only the introduction of the ornate hussar uniform, which was not universally popular. In 1813 *The Public Ledger* condemned it as a 'tiddy dol appearance' which 'would better become an equestrian performer on one of our inferior stages', and *The Statesman* in January 1815 described it as 'a mere gee-gaw … subject, by its intrinsic frivolity, to public ridicule'.

Household regiments

Of the three Household regiments, the 1st and 2nd Life Guards were formed as ordinary regiments only in 1788; earlier they had been styled Horse Guards or 'Life Guard of Horse', membership of which was regarded as a significant step on the social ladder for the offspring of City merchants (hence, it was said,

Badges and accoutrement plates usually bore regimental insignia: this gilt badge, bearing the common motto 'Pro Aris et Focis', was worn upon the side of the Tarleton helmet, probably by the East Riding Yeomanry, c. 1803.

the regimental nickname 'The Cheesemongers'). The Duke of York described them as 'the most useless and unmilitary Troops that ever were seen … nothing but a collection of London Tradespeople', but upon the formation of the Life Guards in 1788 the 'private gentlemen' were mostly discharged and replaced by regularly enlisted troopers, many from the disbanded Horse Grenadiers, previously attached to the Horse Guards. The bad reputation lingered at least until 1808, when the *Morning Chronicle* somewhat maliciously recalled Lord North's witticism regarding the old Horse Guards, that 'the only service he knew them to perform, was kissing the Nursery-maids, and drinking the Children's milk in the Park!' The third Household regiment (though this status was not confirmed officially until March 1820) was the Royal Horse Guards or 'Blues', a suffix added officially to the regimental title as early as 1750, derived from their blue coats which were unique among the heavy cavalry.

'Netherlands' indicates the 1793–95 campaign. Listed in order of seniority:

1st Life Guards: so titled 1788; Peninsula from 1812, Waterloo.

2nd Life Guards: so titled 1788; Peninsula from 1812, Waterloo.

Royal Horse Guards or The Blues: raised 1661; Netherlands, Peninsula from 1812, Waterloo.

1st (King's) Dragoon Guards: raised 1685; Netherlands, Waterloo.

2nd Queen's Dragoon Guards (Queen's Bays): raised 1685; Netherlands.

3rd (Prince of Wales's) Dragoon Guards: raised 1685; Netherlands, Peninsula from 1809.

4th Royal Irish Dragoon Guards: raised 1685; Peninsula 1811–13.

5th Dragoon Guards (from 1804, Princess Charlotte of Wales's): raised 1685; Netherlands, Ireland 1798, Peninsula from 1811.

6th Dragoon Guards (Carabiniers): raised 1685; Netherlands, South America 1807.

7th (Princess Royal's) Dragoon Guards: raised 1688; home service throughout.

1st (Royal) Dragoons: raised 1661; Netherlands, Peninsula from 1809, Waterloo.

2nd (Royal North British) Dragoons (known as Scots Greys): raised 1678; Netherlands, Waterloo.

3rd (King's Own) Dragoons: raised 1685; Walcheren, Peninsula from 1811.

4th Queen's Own Dragoons: raised 1685; Peninsula from 1809.

5th (Royal Irish) Dragoons: raised 1689; Ireland 1798; disbanded 1799.

6th (Inniskilling) Dragoons: raised 1689; Netherlands, Waterloo.

7th Queen's Own Light Dragoons (Hussars from 1806): raised 1690; Netherlands, North Holland 1799, Peninsula 1808–09, 1813–14, Waterloo.

8th (King's Royal Irish) Light Dragoons: raised 1693; Netherlands, Cape 1796–1801, Egypt 1801–02, India thereafter.

9th Light Dragoons: raised 1715; Ireland 1798 (86 years unbroken service in Ireland, ending only 1803), South America 1806, Walcheren, Peninsula 1811–13.

10th Prince of Wales's Own Light Dragoons (Hussars from 1806, Prince of Wales's Own Royal from 1811): raised 1715; Peninsula 1808–09, 1813–14, Waterloo.

11th Light Dragoons: raised 1715; Netherlands, North Holland 1799, Egypt 1801, Hanover 1805, Peninsula 1811–13, Waterloo.

12th (Prince of Wales's) Light Dragoons: raised 1715; Mediterranean (serving as marines) from 1795, Portugal 1797–1800, Egypt 1801, Walcheren, Peninsula from 1811, Waterloo.

13th Light Dragoons: raised 1715; West Indies 1796–98, Peninsula from 1810.

14th Light Dragoons (from 1798 Duchess of York's Own): raised 1715; Netherlands, West Indies 1796–97, Peninsula from 1808, New Orleans.

15th (King's) Light Dragoons (Hussars from 1806): raised 1759; Netherlands, North Holland 1799, Peninsula 1808–09, 1813–14, Waterloo.

16th Queen's Light Dragoons: raised 1759; West Indies 1794, Netherlands, Peninsula from 1809, Waterloo.

17th Light Dragoons: raised 1759; West Indies 1795–97 (including service as marines), Ostend 1798 (detachment), South America 1806–07, then to Cape and India 1808–23.

18th Light Dragoons (King's and Hussars from 1807): raised 1759; West Indies 1795–98, North Holland 1799, Peninsula 1808–09, 1813–14, Waterloo.

19th Light Dragoons: raised 1781 as 23rd, renumbered 1786; India 1782–1807, Niagara frontier 1813–14.

20th Light Dragoons (Jamaica Light Dragoons 1791–1802): raised 1791; West Indies to 1802, Cape and South America 1806, Peninsula 1808, Mediterranean 1805–06, 1808–12, 1814–15, Maida, Egypt 1807, Peninsula (east coast) 1812–13.

21st Light Dragoons (Beaumont's): raised 1794; West Indies 1795–98, Cape 1806–15, South America.

22nd Light Dragoons (Fielding's): raised 1794; Egypt; disbanded 1802. 25th re-numbered 22nd 1802; India, Java.

23rd Light Dragoons (Fullarton's): raised 1794, disbanded 1802. 26th re-numbered 23rd 1802; Peninsula 1808–09, Waterloo.

24th Light Dragoons (Loftus'): raised 1794, disbanded 1802. 27th re-numbered 24th 1802; India.

25th Light Dragoons (known as Gwyn's Hussars): raised 1794; Cape, India, re-numbered 22nd 1802. 29th re-numbered 25th 1802; India.

26th Light Dragoons (Manners'): raised 1795; West Indies 1796–97, Portugal 1798–1800, Egypt 1801; re-numbered 23rd 1802.

27th Light Dragoons (Blathwayt's): raised 1795; Cape, India. Re-numbered 24th 1802.

28th (Duke of York's) Light Dragoons (Lawrie's): raised 1795; West Indies, Cape; disbanded 1802.

29th Light Dragoons (Heathfield's): raised 1795; West Indies, Cape; re-numbered 25th 1802.

30th Light Dragoons (Carden's): raised 1795, drafted 1796.

31st Light Dragoons (St. Leger's): raised 1795, drafted 1796.

32nd Light Dragoons (Blake's): raised 1795, drafted 1796.

33rd (Ulster) Light Dragoons (Blackwood's): raised 1795, drafted 1796.

Heavy cavalry officer's waist belt plate; gilt with silvered devices.

The Tarleton helmet, worn by the light cavalry through almost the entire period; this example bears the red velvet turban and silvered fittings of the East Lothian Yeomanry.

King's German Legion

Among the best and most professional corps in the army, the King's German Legion was formed in 1803 from the king's Hanoverian subjects dispossessed of their lands by French invasion. Latterly Hanoverian recruits were not obtained easily, so other nationalities (and some British officers) were admitted. The Legion included five cavalry regiments, each of four squadrons (five squadrons 1812–14), the 1st and 2nd Dragoons and 1st–3rd Light Dragoons (known as Hussars); in 1813 the Dragoons were re-titled as Light Dragoons and the previous Light Dragoons were officially re-titled as Hussars.

Foreign Corps

A number of regiments formed from French émigrés and foreign mercenaries existed during the Revolutionary Wars, but were not re-formed after the Peace of Amiens. Later foreign cavalry units were few, most notably the hussars of the Brunswick 'Black Legion' which served in the Peninsula. Foreigners also served in British regiments, European musicians and Negro trumpeters in particular being highly valued; the 10th Light Dragoons, for example, included men from Hanover, Austria, Hungary, Holland, France, Africa and the West Indies. In some cases it appears that Negroes were acceptable only as trumpeters: one African was discharged due to a reduction in his regiment's trumpeters as he was regarded as ineligible for service in the ranks; and after 21 years' service (from age 16) another, from St. Kitts, was discharged after the loss of his front teeth prevented him from blowing his trumpet.

Fencibles

The fencible regiments were regular corps whose men were enlisted on the understanding that they would not be sent out of the country in which they were raised, although a number volunteered to extend their service and some fought in the 1798 rebellion in Ireland. They were of considerable value in releasing regular corps for service abroad, but took some potential recruits from the regular army and did not enjoy a universally high reputation. In the House of Commons in November 1795, for example, General McLeod described them as 'a useless body of men ... raised for the purpose of patronage, more than for any service they could be to the country', and Tarleton thought that 'they might be very good to cut a figure in a country village'. Although these views are probably unjustifiably harsh, they were involved in some unfortunate incidents; the Cambridgeshire Light Dragoons were embroiled in an appalling drunken riot in Duns in August 1795, for example, the Pembroke and Cinque Ports behaved with brutality when suppressing the anti-militia riot at

Tranent in 1797, and the Ancient British gained a reputation for barbarity during the 1798 rebellion in Ireland.

The following regiments were raised in 1794, in order of formation, of six troops each unless stated otherwise in parentheses: 1st Regt. or Villiers'; Ancient British (originally styled North Wales Regt.); Lancashire; Rutland; Sussex (1 troop); Duke of York's Own New Romney (2); Cambridgeshire (1); Somersetshire; Loyal Essex; Cornwall (4, increased to 6 1795); Midlothian (2); Norfolk; Berwickshire (2, increased to 4 1795); Princess of Wales's Durham (4); Surrey; Cinque Ports; Berkshire or Windsor Foresters; Hampshire (2); Roxburgh (Roxburgh & Selkirk from 1798; 2, increased to 4 1795); Ayr (2, increased to 6 1796); Dumfries (2, increased to 4 1794); Dumbarton (Lanark & Dumbarton from 1796; 1, increased to 2 1794); Fife (2, increased to 4 1794); Linlithgow (1; Lothian East and West from 1796); Perth (2, increased to 6 1796); Pembrokeshire (1, increased to 3 1795); Oxfordshire (2); and Warwickshire (2). In 1795 the following were formed: Princess Royal's Own (4); Lord Roden's (Irish); Lord Glentworth's (Irish); and in 1799 six regiments of Provisional Cavalry (an abortive attempt to form a cavalry militia) were converted to Fencibles (Berkshire, Kent, Northumberland, Somerset, Suffolk and Worcestershire). All were disbanded in March 1800.

Despite their imperfections, however, the fencibles did provide a useful training-ground for the regulars, as by April 1800 some 1,700 had volunteered for regular service, and at least 105 known ex-fencibles served in the cavalry at Waterloo.

Yeomanry

The part-time volunteer force raised for home defence included a large number of troops of volunteer cavalry or 'gentlemen and yeomanry', which describes their composition: gentry and their outdoor servants, and members of the agricultural or urban business communities sufficiently affluent to provide their own horses. Although a guard against invasion, the duties they actually performed were the prevention or suppression of civil unrest, relieving regular troops from the task. In December 1803 some 33,992 men were enrolled in 604 troops in mainland Britain, but the force's use as a source of basic military training was probably negligible, as a very small proportion ultimately joined the regular army.

Organization

Cavalry regiments were organised in troops, two of which formed at squadron. At the beginning of the Revolutionary Wars the regimental establishment of about 220 of all ranks was increased to about 530, in nine troops, but in the 1794 campaign, excluding the 1st Dragoon Guards, regiments maintained the prewar six-troop establishment, of which two were left at home as a depot squadron. A typical establishment was that of the 4th Dragoon Guards in 1798: one colonel, two lieutenant-colonels, two majors, six captains, one captain-lieutenant, eight lieutenants, nine cornets, one paymaster, one adjutant, one surgeon and two assistants, and one veterinary surgeon; and nine troops, each of one quartermaster, four sergeants, four corporals, one trumpeter and 85 privates. Troops were commanded by the captains, one of the lieutenant-colonels and one of the majors; the ninth, officially commanded by the colonel, was led by the captain-lieutenant. Regimental establishments varied: at this date, for example, the 2nd Dragoon Guards had only eight troops of 70 privates each. In 1803 extra captains were added to relieve

A typical example of regimentally issued medal: a silver example awarded by Lt.Col. Patrick Maxwell of the 19th Light Dragoons, 1801.

field officers of the responsibility of commanding troops; troop quartermasters were converted to troop sergeant-majors from June 1809, and a commissioned quartermaster was added to the regimental staff.

In 1800 regimental establishment was increased to ten troops, two forming the depot, so that four squadrons of two troops each took the field, reduced in 1811 to six 'service' troops. Light regiments maintained ten troops, increased to twelve in September 1813, two acting as the depot. On occasion detachments might serve independently; for example, in 1806–07 part of the 20th Light Dragoons served at the Cape and in South America, and the remainder in Sicily and Egypt, with one troop in the Calabrian expedition. The Life Guards were organised originally in five troops of three companies of 50 men each; the term 'squadron' was used later in the conventional sense to prevent confusion, and a sixth troop was added to both regiments, albeit briefly, in 1799. In order to leave sufficient numbers at home for ceremonial duty, when the Household Cavalry was sent to the Peninsula in 1812, only two squadrons of each regiment were sent abroad, and a similar expedient was applied in the Life Guards for the Waterloo campaign.

The rigours of active service often resulted in strengths lower than the establishment. At the beginning of the Corunna campaign, for example (October 1808), average regimental strength was 615; at the beginning of the 1809 campaign, 385; at Salamanca, 354; at the start of the Vittoria campaign, 412; and at Waterloo (including wounded men still present in the ranks) 441.

CLOTHING AND EQUIPMENT

Although the issue of clothing and equipment was governed by official regulations, the actual provision of such items was not. The cost of some (the 'necessaries') was deducted from the soldiers' pay; but most items were bought by or on behalf of the colonel from private contractors, using money paid to him by the government, hence the differences evident between the equipment of one regiment and another.

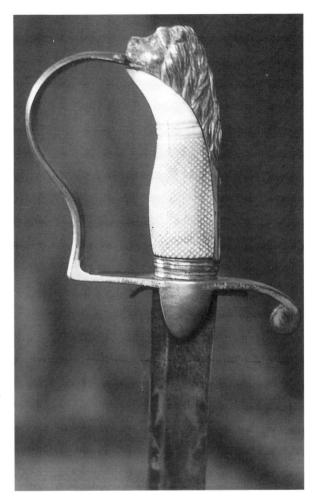

An officer's variety of the 1796 light cavalry sabre, the gilded hilt with a lion head pommel and a chequered ivory grip.

Swords

The sword was the cavalry's principal weapon, but opinions on the most effective design and method of employment were diverse. Almost certainly the most effective sword was a straight-bladed weapon designed to execute the thrust, rather than a curved or broad, straight blade made for the cut or slash. Although British cavalry swords were designed for the cut, many experienced officers advocated the thrusting blade. For example, writing in the *United Service Journal* in 1831 concerning the Peninsular War, 'An Officer of Dragoons' quoted the influential *Reveries* of Marshal Maurice de Saxe (1696–1750) who advocated that the sword should be '*carefully blunted* on the edges, that the soldier may be effectually prevented cutting with it in action, which method of using the sword never does execution . . . There can be no doubt that thrusting is the proper use to make of the sword; it is a brutal operation; that is not our business; let those who make war look to this and much more. We only wish to see our cavalry efficient . . .'

Conversely, an 11th Light Dragoon who was involved in a savage mêlée wrote in the same publication in 1840 that the cut was more effective, being destructive of morale, describing that with cuts to the Frenchmen's heads, 'the appearance presented by these mangled wretches was hideous . . . as far as appearances can be said to operate in rendering men timid, or the reverse, the wounded among the French were thus far more revolting than the wounded among ourselves'. Nevertheless, he admitted the dreadful power of the French thrusting sword after seeing his corporal run through the head.

Originally, commanding officers were permitted to purchase whatever type of sword they desired to arm their regiment, until in 1788 two standardised patterns were introduced. The heavy cavalry weapon

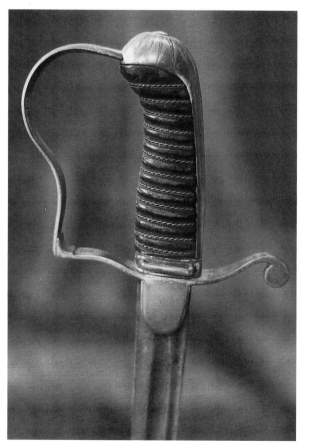

was copied from the existing pattern of the 6th Dragoons, having a spear-pointed 39-inch blade and an iron semi-basket hilt, as shown in Plate B; that for light cavalry had a 36-inch, slightly curved blade and an iron, single-bar stirrup hilt, as in Plate F. The imperfections in these patterns became obvious in the Netherlands in 1794–95, especially when compared with the sabres of Britain's Austrian allies; for example, it was found that the hilt of the heavy sabres so unbalanced the blade that many men and their mounts were injured by their own weapons when attempting to slash at the enemy. Consequently, new weapons were designed by John Gaspard Le Marchant, probably the most forward-thinking British cavalry officer of the era, producing the 1796 patterns which were carried for the remainder of the period.

The 1796 heavy cavalry sabre (Plate B) was copied from the Austrian 1775 pattern for heavy cavalry, which Le Marchant must have seen in the Netherlands; its wide 35-inch blade was double-edged for only 12 inches nearest the tip, and until the hatchet-point was ground into a spear shape, which apparently occurred only in 1815, it could not be used for thrusting. It had a single knuckle-bow and disc-shaped guard pierced with holes. The 'Officer of Dragoons' quoted above dismissed it as 'a lumbering, clumsy, ill-contrived machine. It is too heavy, too short, too broad, too much like the sort of weapon with which we have seen Grimaldi cut off the heads of a line of urchins on the stage'. The 1796 light cavalry sabre (Plate F) had a blade much more curved than that of 1788, much broader and 33 inches long (measured in a straight line from hilt to point), with a curved iron knuckle-bow. It could only really be used for the slash, and the 'Officer of Dragoons' condemned it as being 'constructed in utter defiance of Marshal Saxe . . . as nearly as possible the reverse of what he suggests. We can answer for its utility in making billets for the fire'. Both the 1796 sabres had iron scabbards with suspension rings for use with a waistbelt, resulting in the abandoning of the previous shoulder belt.

An unusual officer's variety of the 1796 light cavalry sabre, the gilded hilt with a slot above the langet to accommodate the sword knot, and a black leather grip bound with gilt wire; the blade has a double fuller. Weapons so different from the regulation pattern can sometimes only be identified by the presence of regimental markings or, as in this case, the name of the maker.

The 1788 regulations were the first to order that officers should carry swords like those of the other ranks, but many regimental and individual variations existed, as shown in Plate F. For example, the 15th Light Dragoons' officers may have used for some years after 1788 an almost straight sword with 'expanding' hilt, two hinged bars folding out from the knuckle-bow to form a semi-basket hilt, a pattern also used by Austria. A distinctive pattern with flat-topped pommel was used by some light regiments as late as 1801 (Plate F), and a popular fashion among light dragoons was the mameluke-hilted sabre with narrow, unfullered *shamshir* or *kilij* blade, popularised by the 1801 Egyptian campaign. Many officers' varieties of the 1796 light cavalry sabre had decorated blades and fishskin grips bound with wire (and sometimes *shamshir* blades, including one with the identification of the 16th Light Dragoons), and some more elaborate patterns existed, such as that of the 10th Light Dragoons with large langets bearing the Prince of Wales's crest (Plate F11).

The 1796 heavy cavalry officers' sword had a blade similar to that of the other ranks, but generally decorated (often blued and gilded), and a semi-basket guard with pierced scroll decoration and slots in the knucklebow which have led to the style being described as 'ladder-hilted'; Plate B8. When not on mounted duty officers had carried light-bladed small-swords (perhaps also used by sergeants in some regiments), originally regimental patterns, perhaps resembling the 1786 infantry spadroon with straight blade, stirrup hilt and cushion-shaped pommel. The practice was recognised officially in 1796 with the introduction of a dress sword for officers of heavy cavalry, not unlike the 1796 infantry sword but with straight quillons and a boat-shaped shell-guard (Plate B10).

Other ranks of the Household Cavalry carried the sabre of the heavy cavalry (examples of the 1796 pattern are known with regimental markings), but another pattern exists which may have been used from about 1808, perhaps only for ceremonial occasions, like the 1796 sabre but with a brass semi-basket

hilt with triangular and half-moon spaces cut out, and a brass scabbard with a frog-hook for suspension (Plate B11). Household Cavalry officers appear to have carried straight-bladed, basket-hilted swords until the adoption of the 1796 ladder-hilted pattern. These appear to have been used by the 1st Life Guards, at least in some orders of dress, at least until 1817, but a new pattern was introduced, perhaps as early as 1805, carried at least by officers of the Royal Horse Guards. Sometimes (and perhaps erroneously) termed the 1814 pattern, it was a Prussian-style *Pallasch* with double-fullered straight blade and a semi-basket hilt made of scroll-shaped bars with a panel bearing the royal crest (a crowned lion atop a large crown) in relief; Plate B12.

When considering the merits of sword-design, it is easy to overlook the brutality of the employment of

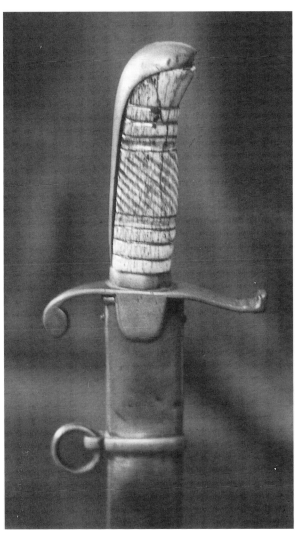

An officer's variety of the 1796 light cavalry sabre with gilded hilt and scabbard and bone grip, with a contemporary conversion in the removal of the knuckle bow to produce a fashionable 'mameluke'-style hilt.

Few contemporary illustrations show the appalling nature of wounds inflicted with a cavalry sabre, but an idea may be gauged from this portrait of Thomas Brown of the King's Own Dragoons, a hero of an earlier war: in capturing a standard at Dettingen he sustained nine fearful injuries. (Print after L.P. Boitard)

stripped them in the night . . . he was lying on his face, his naked body weltering in blood, and as soon as he was turned up, the Officer knew him, he gave a sort of scream, and sprung off his horse, dashed his helmet on the ground, knelt by the body, took the bloody hand and kissed it many times in an agony of grief; it was an affecting and awful scene . . .'

Lances

The lance was a fearsome weapon against infantry, as testified by the destruction of Colborne's brigade at Albuera; but despite its adoption by the British cavalry in 1816, in general it was not highly regarded. One commentator, writing in the *United Service Journal* in 1834, noted of the action at Genappes in 1815 that 'the long unwieldy two-handed lance, at all times ridiculous on horseback, is totally useless the moment you close with the gewgaw champion who bears it', a common opinion. Apparently the only British forces to use the lance during the period were the émigré corps of Uhlans Britanniques or Bouille's, 1793–96.

Firearms

At the beginning of the French Revolutionary Wars three main patterns of cavalry carbine were in use. Heavy cavalry carried the 1770 heavy dragoon pattern, similar to the infantry musket but with a smaller bore, 42-inch barrel, bayonet and the usual side-bar affixed to the stock (on the reverse side of the lock) which enabled the weapon to be suspended from the spring-clip of a shoulder-belt. Light cavalry carried the Light Dragoon or Elliott pattern, designed by Gen. George Augustus Elliott (Lord Heathfield), colonel of the 15th Light Dragoons 1759–90; this had a 28-inch barrel and a catch to hold the ramrod in place. Approved in 1773, it was still in use in the mid-1840s, when the barrels were reduced to 20 ins. and the weapons re-issued to yeomanry; later examples had provision for a bayonet. The Royal Horse Guards carried the 'Blues carbine' with a 37-inch barrel and a superior quality of lock. There was also Harcourt's carbine, named after Gen. William Harcourt (3rd Earl Harcourt, colonel of the 16th Light Dragoons 1779–1830), supplied in 1794 but of uncertain pattern.

The Board of General Officers reported in 1796 that the heavy dragoon carbine was unduly cumber-

such weapons. An eye-witness account (in *The Courier*, 20 April 1811) of the killing of Col. Chamorin of the French 26th Dragoons by Cpl. Logan of the 13th Light Dragoons illustrates the point:

'. . . this corporal had killed one of his men, and he was so enraged, that he sallied out himself and attacked the corporal – the corporal was well mounted and a good swordsman, as was also the Colonel – both defended for some time, the corporal cut him twice in the face, his helmet came off at the second, when the corporal slew him by a cut which nearly cleft his skull asunder, it cut in as deep as the nose through the brain'. Next day, a wounded French officer came under flag of truce to retrieve the body: '. . . it was truly a bloody scene, being almost all sabre wounds, the slain were all naked, the peasants having

some, and recommended that until a new weapon with a 26-inch barrel could be issued, existing weapons should be cut down to this length, and that a 'swivel bar' be added to permit it to be carried butt-downwards. From 1797 some carbines were equipped with Henry Nock's so-called 'screwless lock', in which the mechanism was concealed within the stock, behind the lock-plate. This high-quality lock had been designed at the instigation of the Duke of Richmond when he was Master-General of the Ordnance in 1786, and intended for an abortive infantry musket; unused locks were re-issued and fitted to the carbines of some regiments, for example the 16th Light Dragoons and 2nd Dragoon Guards. So good were these mechanisms that the latter regiment was still using the original issue in 1832, having suffered hardly any breakdowns.

From about late 1808 the Paget carbine was issued to light cavalry, named after Gen. Henry Paget (later Earl of Uxbridge and Marquess of Anglesey), who may have been involved with its design. It had a 16-inch barrel, a 'bolt lock' incorporating a sliding safety-catch, and a swivel ramrod to prevent its being lost when loading on horseback. A singular variant had a hinged, folding stock, conceivably a regimental conversion by the 16th Light Dragoons.

Some Baker rifled carbines were issued, apparently from 1803, in limited numbers (they were carried by the 10th Light Dragoons, for example). Originally they resembled the infantry Baker rifle, with scrolled brass trigger-guard (an example dated 1805 is known, bearing the mark of the 7th Light Dragoons), but an improved stock was designed with a pistol-style grip providing a better fitting for the hand; an issue of these was made to the 10th in late 1813. Presumably rifled carbines were used by men designated as 'flankers' or skirmishers, if not carried by entire regiments.

Carbines were not especially effective, and probably the lack of importance placed upon skirmishing and 'outpost' duty inhibited attempts to design better ones. Jonathan Leach of the 95th, writing about the Peninsular War, remarked that the 'little pop-gun of

a carbine' was so inferior to that of the French that the enemy often dismounted 'and shot at our dragoons at a distance which rendered our short carbines almost useless'. The rifled carbines were better: 'Fluellyn' in the *United Service Journal* (1840) stated that during the Peninsular War, 'the rifle-carbines served out to the Hussar skirmishers proved little, if at all, inferior to the long, infantry fusil', but these were the exception; in fact in 1813 Stapleton Cotton ordered carbines to be withdrawn from the Household Cavalry, except for six per troop, as these men were not expected to skirmish and were sufficiently encumbered already. The 'Officer of Dragoons' was suitably dismissive: 'Our heavy dragoon carbine is pretty efficient ... our light dragoon carbine is so decidedly bad in all respects, that we have only patience to say, the sooner it is got rid of the better ... We never saw a pistol made use of except to shoot a glandered horse.'

Nevertheless, a number of patterns of pistol were used, generally distinguished by dimensions of barrel and bore. The varieties in use at the beginning of the Revolutionary Wars included the heavy dragoon pattern (12 in. barrel, in both carbine- and pistol-bore); light dragoon (9 in. barrel, carbine-bore); Life Guards (10 in. barrel, carbine-bore); and Royal Horse Guards (10 in. barrel, pistol-bore). All appear to have had brass butt-caps and a brass-shod wooden ramrod. In addition, during the 1790s the Ordnance purchased large quantities from the East India Company, a source of supply used to supplement those from government contractors as late as 1813.

In 1796 the Board of General Officers recom-

A trooper of the 13th Light Dragoons, executing the guard or parry with the sabre. This shows the 1812 light dragoon uniform with dress shabraque; note the short-barrelled Paget carbine. (Aquatint by I.C. Stadler after Charles Hamilton Smith, published April 1812)

mended a new universal pistol, one to be carried by each man, with a 9-inch barrel of musket-bore and an iron ramrod carried in the holster; the furniture was reduced to just a brass trigger guard (no butt-plate), and some were fitted with Nock's lock. It was not popular and was modified by the attachment of an ordinary or swivel ramrod, and by 1801 the previous light dragoon pattern was again being ordered from government contractors. From about 1810 'raised pans' became common (an attempt to make the priming-pan waterproof), and many weapons were converted by the addition of such improvements as locking-bolts and swivel ramrods. Despite the obvious advantages, the 1796 attempt to standardise the bore was abandoned, so that pistols continued to exist in both pistol- and carbine-bore, perhaps partly to prevent accidents: using a cartridge common to both, a full charge of powder suitable for a carbine would have caused dangerous recoil in a pistol. Not until 1828 was the withdrawal of the cavalry pistol recommended officially, and as late as 1837 it was still being condemned as a useless encumbrance.

Officers carried privately purchased pistols of much finer workmanship, including such curiosities as the double-barrelled pistol with a single trigger carried by Capt. Williams of the 7th Light Dragoons in the Peninsula, which a fellow officer condemned as a most dangerous thing. (Double-barrelled pistols with detachable shoulder stocks were ordered from Henry Nock for the Royal Horse Artillery in 1793, but although such weapons may have been used in small numbers by yeomanry – the Norfolk Rangers, for example, used something similar – they were not carried by regular cavalry.)

Artillery

Light fieldpieces could be attached to cavalry regiments, but these 'galloper guns' were used normally only in India, and even then not by all: for example, 'Black Jack' Vandeleur of the 8th Light Dragoons repeatedly refused them, saying that 'the 8th must depend on their good swords and their own innate bravery' (he was killed at Laswaree, 1803).

Uniforms

Heavy cavalry wore bicorn hats and red tail-coats with open, facing-coloured lapels until 1796, when

Above: The Austrian sword-exercise (with a sabre in each hand), performed by a Mr. Goldham of the Loyal London Cavalry, showing the manner of standing in the stirrups. (Mezzotint by S. W. Reynolds after D. Wolstenholme)

Left: Training: the sword-exercise performed on horseback by troopers of the Warwickshire Yeomanry. (Engraving by C. Williams after E. Rudge, 1801)

they were closed to the waist, and made single-breasted and without lapels in 1797. Light dragoons wore the fur-crested 'Tarleton' helmet, and a blue, braided, sleeved wasitcoat with a sleeveless, short-tailed blue shell-jacket over the top, until in 1796 a sleeved blue jacket was adopted (French-grey for regiments serving in India or at the Cape). Items of hussar uniform, including furred pelisses, were worn by some light dragoon regiments even before being made official for those regiments converted to hussars. New uniforms were introduced (to considerable criticism) in 1812: for the heavy cavalry, a single-breasted red jacket and maned leather helmet, prompting the *Royal Military Chronicle* in the following January to liken the new uniform to 'a sort of modern antique without a similarity, unless, indeed, in the older wardrobes of some of the theatres'; and for light dragoons, broad-topped shakos and blue, Polish-style jackets of such French style that Wellington lamented upon the confusion caused (the *Chronicle* remarked that the uniforms must have been 'altered and altered till no English alteration remained, and it was therefore necessary to adopt French ones').

The bicorn hat was not especially functional, warping out of shape after exposure to weather; those of the 1st Dragoons in the Peninsula were compared unfavourably to dustmen's hats, and they had worn decrepit clothing for so long that it was decided not to issue new clothing all at once lest their unusually smart appearance prevented them from being recognised! The handsome 'Tarleton' helmet was hot to wear and also warped; Tomkinson of the 16th Light Dragoons described them as 'bad things for a soldier ... the first rain puts them out of shape'. The Board of General Officers in 1796 reported them as unsuitable for tropical climates, recommending instead tin helmets lined with white linen; the resulting crested, maned helmets bore regimental badges on the front such as the harp of the 8th Light Dragoons or the alligator of the 20th. The fur hussar busbies were top-heavy and frequently fell off, provided no protection, and having pasteboard interiors soaked up the wet and became unbearably heavy; latterly some were replaced by shakos.

No use was made of body-armour, save for a brief issue of old iron cuirasses (and perhaps skull-caps for wear inside the hat like the 'secrete' of the 17th century) to the Royal Horse Guards for the Netherlands campaign of 1793–94; the cuirasses were found to be cumbersome and soon went rusty, so were returned to store. Part of the 2nd Life Guards wore black-enamelled cuirasses (with gilded ornaments for officers) at a review in 1814, but they were discontinued immediately. The old buff-leather protective coat had long passed out of use (the last to wear it was apparently Col. Preston of the Scots Greys in the Seven Years' War), but as an example of the type of unofficial equipment adopted by officers, Thomas Brotherton of the 14th Light Dragoons wore a buffalo-hide cuirass in the Peninsula in 1812–13, to protect the place where he had been run-through the body at Salamanca. Gauntlets were not part of light

Sword-exercises. (From Rules and Regulations for the Sword Exercise of Cavalry, *1796.) The picture to the left is of the 'Guard'. The right hand picture is of the cut against infantry. Only against infantry was it permitted to bend the elbow when delivering a blow; against cavalry the elbow was kept rigid so as not to expose it to a counter-blow, all movement coming from the wrist and shoulder.*

dragoon uniform, but he wore some sufficiently thick to prevent the loss of a finger when a Frenchman slashed at him.

Swords were carried on shoulder belts until June 1796, when waist belts with slings were used, generally wide belts for heavy regiments and narrow for light. In November 1796 it was specified that regiments with buff facings should use buff leather-work, the others white, and that the few light dragoon regiments which had adopted red morocco belts should use them only until the current issue was worn out. Thereafter, shoulder belts were restricted to those supporting the pouch and carbine. Other items carried over the shoulder such as haversacks and canteens were of the type common to the remainder of the army.

Horses

The introduction of light cavalry in the mid-18th century caused a fundamental change in the type of cavalry horse. The usual troop-horse had been a heavy black animal ('black horse' previously referred to a generic type of heavy charger, not just the colour), but civilian horse-breeding in the later 18th century produced lighter hunters and speedier carriage-horses. The Board of General Officers convened in 1796 to enquire into all aspects of cavalry service reported that the previous 'black' was either extinct or 'reformed' by selective breeding, and replaced by a lighter animal bred originally to pull gentlemen's carriages. Consequently, heavy regiments were permitted to ride other colours than black, although some regiments continued to use blacks exclusively for some time, for example the 1st

Dragoon Guards and 1st Dragoons, and the 3rd Dragoons were mounted entirely on blacks until 1811. The Household regiments always retained blacks; light cavalry had ridden horses of different colours probably from their creation. The 2nd Dragoon Guards rode all bays (hence the title 'Queen's Bays'), and the 2nd Dragoons greys (hence 'Scots Greys').

The docking of horses' tails was abandoned in 1764, but in 1799 it was ordered that except for the Household regiments, heavy cavalry horses should have 'nag', 'switch' or 'cock-tails', trimmed to a shorter length. In some regiments horses were allocated to squadrons according to colour, and tail-length varied accordingly: in 1798, for example, troopers in the 1st Dragoon Guards rode long-tailed blacks, trumpeters long-tailed greys, and officers nag-tailed browns, bays or chestnuts; in the 4th Dragoon Guards two squadrons rode long-tailed blacks, the others nag-tailed bays, trumpeters greys, and officers short-tailed bays; and in the 5th Dragoon Guards both officers and men rode nag-tailed dark and bright bays, and trumpeters greys. Greys were notably distinctive, hence their use by trumpeters, but were not favoured by officers in case they were singled-out by the enemy; although it was remarked that Lt. Standish O'Grady of the 7th Hussars was the only officer of that regiment to ride a conspicuous grey at Waterloo, and was the only officer from the regiment whose horse and person emerged un-scathed. At Laswaree the entire 8th Light Dragoons were mounted on 'white' horses, the property of the King of Oudh, except for the colonel, Thomas Pakenham Vandeleur (alias 'Black Jack'), who rode his own black racehorse.

Most horses were bred and purchased in Britain as those from the countries in which the army campaigned were generally not suitable: the local breeds of the Iberian peninsula, for example, were too small and not available in sufficient numbers. The experiment of sending troops abroad without horses was tried with the 20th Light Dragoons in 1808, but abandoned due to the difficulty of procuring mounts in Portugal. Heavy cavalry horses were generally

HERE LIES
COPENHAGEN
THE CHARGER RIDDEN BY
THE DUKE OF WELLINGTON,
THE ENTIRE DAY, AT THE
BATTLE OF WATERLOO.

BORN 1808, DIED 1836.

A typical cavalry mount of the type ridden by officers: a portrait of Wellington's famous horse 'Copenhagen', with his tombstone: 'God's humbler instrument though meaner clay/Should share the glory of that glorious day', sentiments appropriate for all the army's horses.

Training: sword exercises, c.1805

A

Heavy cavalry equipment
1: 1812 pattern dragoon helmet
2: Shoulder belt with the 1788 sabre
3: Waist belt with 1796 heavy cavalry sabre
4: Waist belt plate, King's Dragoon Guards

5: Plate worn on shoulder belt of 1st Dragoon Guards officer
6: Plate worn on shoulder belt of 3rd Dragoon Guards officer
7: Plate worn on shoulder belt of 4th Dragoon Guards officer
8: 1788 heavy cavalry sabre
9: 1796 heavy cavalry sabre
10: 1796 officer's dress sword

11: 1796 style sabre, Household Cavalry
12: Officer's dress sabre, Household Cavalry
13: 1796 pattern officer's sabre
14: Heavy dragoon carbine
15: Fitting for suspending carbine from belt
16: Flintlock mechanism

17: Flints and cartridges
18: 1796 pattern carbine
19: 1796 pattern carbine with Nock's enclosed lock
20: Heavy dragoon pistol
21: 1796 pattern pistol

10th Hussars in camp, 1815

C

4th Dragoons on the march, c.1809-11

D

Horse Furniture
1: Heavy cavalry saddlery and equipment
2: Horse furniture of a trooper of the
   13th Light Dragoons, 1812

3: Officer's full dress furniture, 4th Dragoons
4: Officer's full dress furniture,
   15th Hussars, c.1813

5: 1805 light cavalry or Hussar saddle
6: Heavy cavalry saddle
7: Officer's light cavalry shabraque,
   23rd Light Dragoons

8: Valise-ends a: 15th King's Hussars
   b: 1st Royal Dragoons
   c: 3rd Troop, 2nd Dragoons

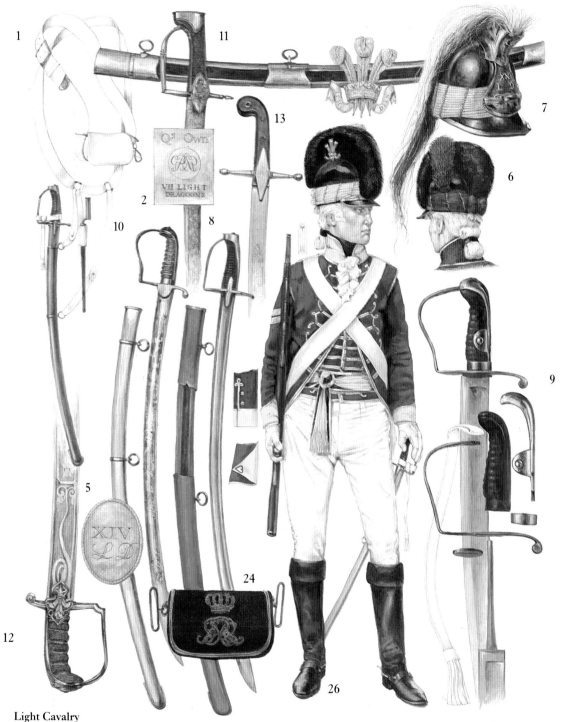

Light Cavalry
1: Shoulder belt and 1788 light cavalry sabre
2: Officer's plate, 7th Light Dragoons
3: Officer's plate, 15th Light Dragoons
4: Officer's plate, London and Westminster
   Light Horse Volunteers
5: Other ranks' plate, 14th Light Dragoons
6: Tarleton helmet, 16th Light Dragoons

7: Tropical helmet, 20th Light Dragoons
8: 1788 pattern light cavalry sabre
9: 1796 pattern light cavalry sabre
10: Officer's 1796 pattern sabre
11: Officer's sabre
12: Officer's sabre, 10th Light Dragoons
13: Officer's non-regulation sabre

14: Elliot carbine
15: Suspension-bar, 1796 carbine
16: Baker rifled carbine
17: Paget carbine
18: Paget suspension-bar
19: 1796 pistol

20: Nock's enclosed lock
21: Light dragoon pistol
22: Modified light dragoon pistol
23: Picker and lock for cleaning a flintlock
24: Hussar officer's pouch

25: Silver plated plug-in spur
26: Sergeant, 10th Light Dragoons, 1790
27: 13th Light Dragoons, 1812
28: 14th Light Dragoons, 1812

G

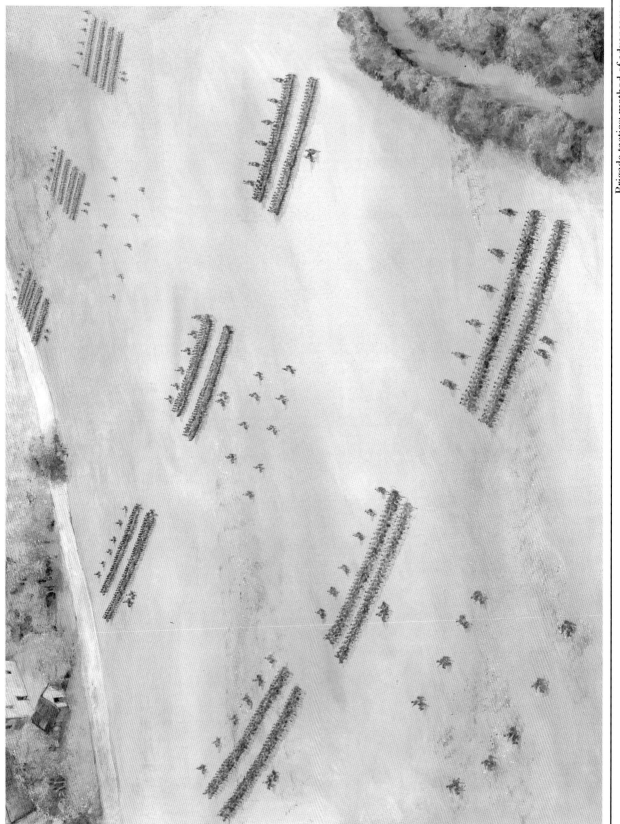

Capture of the French 45th Line 'Eagle', Waterloo

around 15 hands, those of light regiments slightly smaller; for active service, the ideal mounts were five or six years old, costing about £40–45 each. Younger horses were reckoned unsuitable for campaign, and in 1813 Wellington suggested that if newly purchased five to six year-olds were too expensive, older horses from regiments at home should be sent to the Peninsula, and replaced with younger horses for home service, which generally cost about £25 each. However, it was not unknown for worn-out horses to be sent to regiments on campaign, such as the draft received by the 14th Light Dragoons in July 1809 of 61 animals from the Irish Commissariat Corps, already rejected as unfit for heavy cavalry.

Usually each troop-commander was allowed two or three horses (four for the lieutenant-colonel), the other officers one each (though many kept others privately), and one horse per 'other rank' plus five or six extra per troop. Usually more horses were lost in action than riders; an example is provided by the casualties sustained by the 3rd K.G.L. Hussars in their repeated charges at Göhrde (16 September 1813): killed, 13 men, 47 horses; wounded, 69 men, 76 horses; missing, 16 men, 15 horses.

Officers purchased their own horses, or had the colonel purchase them on their behalf, not over £50

Kensington cavalry barracks. (Print after C.R.B. Barrett)

each and with the price deducted from the officer's pay; but all troop-horses were bought by or on behalf of the colonel, a system which could be abused. For example, in 1799 the colonel and lieutenant-colonel of the Sussex Fencible Cavalry (Sir George Thomas Bt. and Christopher Teesdale respectively) were court-martialled for having bought inferior horses at less than the price allowed by the government and then appropriating the difference. Both were acquitted, but after reviewing the evidence the Duke of York (the Commander-in-Chief) stated that the verdict of the court was 'so extraordinary' that had he seen the evidence before the court-martial he would have dismissed Thomas immediately for conduct 'so improper and so unwarrantable', and that at the very least Teesdale was guilty of 'a criminal connivance'. Although the court's decision could not be reversed, the Duke announced publicly that neither officer should ever be allowed again to use government funds to purchase horses.

Instructions were published in 1795 on the care and feeding of horses, and to improve their condition in 1796 veterinary surgeons became regularly commissioned, and a Principal Veterinary Surgeon to the Army was appointed. However, neglect of horses was such that the regulations were repeated in an article in the *British Military Journal* in 1801, which deplored that 'Many horses grow broken winded every year, owing to the troopers being allowed to fill them with water, and giving them as much hay in one day, as would nearly be sufficient for three'. The cause was ascribed to officers believing stable-duty was beneath their dignity, and all were urged to visit the stables at least once a day, and not leave inspections to N.C.O.s. It was always necessary to supervise the daily feeds to ensure that no unscrupulous troopers sold their horses' rations to buy alcohol, and during the Peninsular War it was believed that the extra care

Croydon cavalry barracks: a barrack-block. (Print after C.R.B. Barrett)

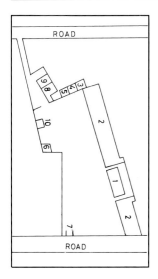

Plan of St. Gregory's cavalry barracks, Canterbury, 1794. Key: (1) barracks for 288 men; (2) stabling for 366 horses, with rooms for 42 men and store-rooms above; (3) blacksmith's forge; (4) cook-house; (5) cleaning room; (6) offices; (7) lavatory; (8) dung-pit; (9) forage-room; (10) pond.

calculation that for a regiment 400 strong, the total weight of food for horses and men at the regulation rate amounted to over $5\frac{1}{2}$ tons per day; alternative statistics which specified 20 lbs. of hay, 10 lbs. of oats and 5 lbs. of straw per horse per day would have raised this weight by a further $1\frac{1}{4}$ tons.

Hard campaigning could severely affect the ability of the regiment to field all its available horses and men. This is exemplified by a detachment of 30 men of Hompesch's Chasseurs and 20 of Roden's Fencibles in the 1798 rebellion, in the operations before the action at Ballinamuck. After marching 90 miles in 48 hours and three skirmishes with the French and rebel rear-guard, despite having sustained no casualties the detachment was reduced by lameness and fatigue of the horses to 24 men of Hompesch's and 12 of Roden's, a rate of attrition of 28 per cent virtually before a blow was struck. (Nevertheless, the survivors demonstrated the effect which cavalry could have upon unformed or unsteady infantry: as the enemy retired over the bridge at Ballinamuck, they charged the rearguard of 3-400 French infantry and captured the whole body, which threw down its arms just as the troopers began to sabre them.)

given to their mounts by the German Legion was the reason why they invariably appeared to be in better condition.

A horse on home service received a daily ration of 14 lbs. of hay, 10 lbs. of oats and 4 lbs. of straw. On campaign part of the ration was provided by cutting forage locally, but supplies often failed and the condition of mounts declined accordingly: 'Had Don Quixote lived at this time, he might have gone blindfold through our camp; quite certain to have found a Rosinante in any horse on which he first laid his hands. Chopped straw and stagnant water, with constant exposure to a broiling sun, and being picketed under a shadeless tree, reduced them to a pitiable state, and established the well-known furrows down the hind quarters, so strongly indicating poverty and starvation', as Jonathan Leach recalled. The problems of supply may be appreciated from the

Horse furniture

Horse furniture was purchased by the regimental colonel, so initially there was little standardization, although from 1791 the Ordnance department became responsible for the patterns used. Heavy cavalry used stout leather and wood saddles with a goatskin seat, a leather bucket at the right front to take the carbine butt (with the barrel supported by a strap around the pommel), pistol holsters at each side of the pommel and attached to the harness breast-strap (with pistol butts angled backwards), and a rolled cloak or valise behind the saddle. Lighter patterns, similar to civilian hunting saddles, were

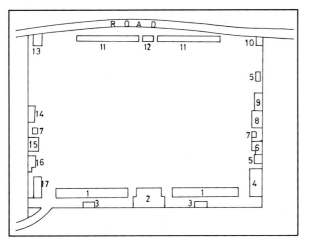

Plan of King's Cavalry Barracks, Canterbury, 1808. Key: (1) stables for 133 horses each, with accommodation above for 146 and 133 men; (2) quarters for 16 officers; (3) cook-houses; (4) riding school; (5) dung-pits; (6) forage barns; (7) granaries; (8) coal yard; (9) hospital-stable for 24 horses; (10) forge; (11) carriage-sheds for 40 and 34 carriages, and blacksmith's and wheelwright's shops; (12) armourer's, tailor's and saddler's shops; (13) guard house; (14) canteen; (15) forage barn, engine house, carpenter's and bricklayer's shops; (16) wash-house; (17) hospital for 36 patients.

'Foreign corps': a cavalry charge executed by the Brunswick 'Black Legion'.

used by light dragoons; among probably many regimental variations was the practice of the 11th Light Dragoons, noted in 1789, of carrying their sabres on the saddle.

Standardization of horse furniture originated with the Duke of York's observations of the Prussian army, and sample sets of Prussian equipment were obtained as models. The resulting 1796 'Heavy Cavalry Universal Saddle' was ordered to be made of brown leather with black harness (though in practice it appears often to have been dark brown), with a four-inch girth, divided crupper, single breast-strap, 'square'-sided stirrups, a brass edging to the cantle (seat rear) to prevent wear, and leather pistol holsters with brass ends, carried on each side of the pommel. The holsters were covered by a rolled cloak secured to the saddle by three straps; at the rear of the seat was a tubular cloth valise, around which was often wrapped the waterdeck, a waterproof sheet of painted canvas some 52 inches square, large enough to cover the whole saddle and bridle when placed on the ground. In July 1796 the decorative shabraque and holster caps were abolished for the rank and file, but are depicted at a later date reserved for full dress; ordinarily a folded blanket was carried beneath the saddle.

The 'Light Cavalry Universal Saddle' (alias 'Hungarian' or 'Hussar' pattern) was designed in 1805, with beech-wood side-boards and front and rear arches, detachable leather flaps, and a leather 'woof' or 'wolf', a rawhide seat which was covered by a quilted leather 'pilch' or cushion attached by loops to the pommel and cantle. Unlike the heavy cavalry saddle, it had no padding on the underside, necessitating the use of a thickly folded blanket to prevent sores on the horse's back. Pistol-holsters were attached at either side of the pommel, and the valise at the rear; stirrups had 'round' sides. A sheepskin saddle cover was often used, with the decorative shabraque reserved for full dress. The use of this saddle was extended to all light cavalry in 1812, but as equipment was replaced only when it wore out, older patterns probably remained in use throughout the period. Carbine-boots, attached to the right of the saddle, by the pistol-holster, latterly accommodated the muzzle instead of the butt. Regimental variations continued in use: for example, the 7th Hussars from late 1813 were among the regiments to use a design of holster invented by the London saddler Laurie, guaranteed not to shake or touch the horse's shoulder, whereas the ordinary pattern, buckled to the breast-strap, was unsteady and could injure the horse by its continual jolting.

Bridles generally featured a double (curb and snaffle) bit, and from 1812 the light cavalry adopted a Hungarian-style bridle with crossed face-straps, similar to those used by hussars earlier, and sometimes including much ornamentation, especially for officers. The halter or head-collar, used for tying up the horse in stables or in the field, was made of leather or webbing, sometimes coloured white, and was carried either bound around the halter neck-strap or running to the nearside of the saddle. It could be dispensed with by using the bridle as a head-collar.

On campaign, horses were frequently loaded with more equipment than the weight they were supposedly able to carry (some 250 lbs. or about one-quarter of body-weight). A leather case containing spare horseshoes was strapped to the offside rear of the saddle (one 7th Hussar officer recorded that he carried spare nails in his cap!), and other equipment could include mallet, tent-pegs and hatchet in a canvas water-bucket at the rear of the saddle, a mess-tin upon the valise, a picket-stake strapped to the carbine (to be discarded before action), corn-sacks across the saddle, a nosebag on the rear offside of the saddle, and sometimes nets of hay.

TYPICAL ENGAGEMENTS

Many of the actions fought by British cavalry during the period are well known, but some of the most significant are worthy of examination.

Villers-en-Cauchies and Le Cateau

The first great exploit of the British cavalry during the period occurred at Villers-en-Cauchies during the Netherlands campaign. On 24 April 1794, in response to a French advance from Cambrai, the Austrian general Ott led some 160 men of the 15th Light Dragoons and 112 men of the Austrian Leopold Hussars (two squadrons of each) as the advance party of his force; the ten squadrons which followed them included General Mansel's brigade of Royal Horse Guards, 3rd Dragoon Guards and 1st Dragoons, with the 11th Light Dragoons and two Austrian cuirassier squadrons. Encountering some French light cavalry, Ott pursued them until they halted, screening a force of some 5,000 French; realizing that his supports were nowhere in evidence, Ott assembled his officers and told them their only course of action was to charge. This they did, the 15th led by Capt. Aylett; when the French cavalry moved aside, unmasking an artillery battery and six infantry battalions. Braving the fire, the 15th swept through the gunners and fell upon the infantry, who fled in total disorder. The French cavalry were broken and pursued by the Austrians while the 15th (now led by Capt. Pocklington, Aylett having fallen) cut up an artillery train and chased them to the town of Bouchain, from which emerged French reinforcements. Bereft of support and unable to carry off the captured guns, Pocklington rallied his men and led them off at a trot, their blue uniforms temporarily confusing the French about their identity. Reaching the village of Villers-en-Cauchies, Pocklington found his escape blocked by French troops; so after driving back the French force now pursuing from Bouchain, he faced-about again and cut his way clear. In this

Cavalry combat: Cpl. Logan of the 13th Light Dragoons engaging Col. Chamorin of the French 26th Dragoons at Campo Mayor, who was killed in the encounter. Though a good representation of a cavalry action, the 1812 light dragoon uniform is shown in error, as the previous pattern with 'Tarleton' helmet was that actually worn. (Aquatint by M. Dubourg after Denis Dighton)

brilliant exploit some 1,200 French troops were killed or wounded, for the loss of 31 men of the 15th and 10 Austrians; and but for the lack of action by Mansel's brigade, a considerable victory would have resulted.

Mansel appears to have led his troops into heavy fire, causing the 3rd Dragoon Guards to break after suffering heavily, their retreat being covered by the 1st Dragoons. Accusations of incompetence and even cowardice so stung Mansel that he resolved not to emerge alive from the next action, which occurred two days later at Le Cateau. Here, Ott led six Austrian and twelve British squadrons against some 20,000 French troops. Concealed by folds in the terrain, Ott formed in three lines (Austrian Zeschwitz Cuirassiers in the first, Mansel's brigade in the second, the 1st and 5th Dragoon Guards and 16th Light Dragoons in the third) and burst upon the French left flank and rear; within moments the entire formation had dissolved and was mercilessly cut-up by the cavalry, losing about 3,400 men and 22 guns. A second French column was dispersed with some 1,200 casualties by a separate force of Austrian hussars and two squadrons each of the 7th and 11th Light Dragoons. Mansel, riding far ahead of his command, was killed in the mêlée. It was perhaps the most convincing demonstration during the period of the effect of a cavalry charge handled well and launched at the correct moment.

The Peninsular War

In the early Peninsular War the terrain was not suitable for the employment of large cavalry forces, and Wellington was inclined to refuse augmentations to his cavalry, until by mid-1811 he declared that he could not have too many. Even including the Portuguese, however, and although the numbers increased, they represented only 8.2 per cent of the army at Salamanca and 10.2 per cent at the start of the Vittoria campaign.

The first example of what Wellington termed 'the trick of galloping at everything' occurred at Vimeiro, where he sent his cavalry (240 men of the 20th Light Dragoons and 260 Portuguese) to pursue some broken French infantry. The Portuguese retired when shot at, but Col. Taylor of the 20th led his men through the infantry and galloped on, until assailed by French cavalry; disordered by the wild charge, they had to gallop back to the British lines,

The capture of French officers by a hussar, who wears the shako adopted in preference to the fur cap in the later stages of the Peninsular War. (Aquatint by M. Dubourg after William Heath)

having lost about one-fifth of their strength and Taylor, who was killed.

Paget gained success at Sahagun (21 December 1808, when the 15th Hussars routed two French regiments) and Benevente (29 December 1808, when the 10th Hussars defeated a smaller French force), but errors emerged again at Talavera. Here, Anson's brigade (23rd Light Dragoons and 1st K.G.L. Hussars) advanced against infantry in square, but were disordered completely by charging too quickly to avoid a ravine concealed by long grass. Those who emerged uninjured should have halted to re-form, but they galloped on; the attempt to break the squares being hopeless, the 1st Hussars and half the 23rd retired, but the 23rd's two right squadrons careered on to engage a cavalry brigade towards the rear of the French position. Outnumbered and surrounded, they were almost annihilated, only seven or eight men escaping from the 170 involved. Although this clearly demonstrated the hazards of the inability to rally, as late as 1831 it was being argued (in the *United Service Journal*) that the charge was a success.

Such incidents have tended to obscure the real value of the cavalry to the Peninsular army, for despite the lack of 'outpost' training, not once did the French manage to mount a surprise attack of the kind inflicted upon them at Foz d'Arouce and Arroyo dos Molinos, and there were only a couple of incidents when British cavalry detachments were caught off-

Cavalry combat at Waterloo, showing British heavy cavalry able to execute a thrust due to the modification to the point of the sabre. (Engraving by R. Havell after I.M. Wright)

guard, one at least due to the incompetence of a newly arrived officer. The value of experienced cavalry is demonstrated by the remarkable achievement of the 1st K.G.L. Hussars who, assisted by the 14th and 16th Light Dragoons, held a 40-mile line for four months in 1810, against four times their number, without losing a vedette, letting through one French scout or sending back one piece of incorrect intelligence.

A noted success occurred at Usagre (25 May 1811), when Gen. Hon. William Lumley, one of the best cavalry brigadiers, ambushed a very strong French cavalry force. Lumley kept his command concealed until two French regiments had crossed the Usagre bridge, and then fell upon them; trapped by the river, these regiments were isolated from support and Lumley was able to destroy them at leisure. Emphasizing the need for an intelligent commander, a similar situation was mishandled by von Bock and George Anson at Villadrigo in October 1812, when the former permitted French cavalry to cross a bridge before he engaged, and had to withdraw when French reinforcements came up.

The classic example of the use of cavalry in a full battle occurred at Salamanca, when Le Marchant was ordered by Wellington in person to 'charge at all hazards' upon a mass of French infantry, already shaken by musketry; no more opportune circumstances existed for a cavalry charge. His three regiments (5th Dragoon Guards and 4th Dragoons, 3rd Dragoons in support) wrecked the left of the French army, and under Le Marchant's direction apparently re-formed during the action, before riding down a column of fresh French troops. As the attack turned into a pell-mell pursuit, Le Marchant rallied a troop of 4th Dragoons as a reserve; it was at the head of these, dispersing a French unit attempting to rally, that Le Marchant was shot and killed.

During the pursuit of the French on the following day, there occurred at Garcia Hernandez that rarest of incidents, the breaking of infantry in square, a formation generally impervious to cavalry attack. Bock's brigade (1st and 2nd K.G.L. Dragoons) approached French infantry, of which the forward elements were in square. As Bock appears to have been caught up in an earlier charge, credit for the attack rests with the squadron commanders. Advancing in echelon, after French fire had disordered the leading squadron, Capt. von der Decken led his following squadron straight at the square. He was mortally wounded by the next volley, but a wounded horse crashed into the side of the square, crushing six or eight files, and into this gap the following dragoons rode. The square dissolved in disorder and most of the Frenchmen surrendered on the spot. The other battalions attempted to escape, but had not time to form square properly and were ridden down by succeeding squadrons.

Conversely, two final examples of Peninsular actions demonstrate the old failings of charges getting out of hand, and the lack of awareness of the importance of maintaining a reserve or rallying after the initial success. The most serious of these was at Maguilla (11 June 1812), involving the lamentable Slade. After driving in some French vedettes with the 3rd Dragoon Guards and 1st Dragoons, Slade was confronted by the French 17th and 27th Dragoons, whose brigade-commander, General Lallemand, had withdrawn a squadron to act as a reserve. Slade attacked with the 1st Dragoons in the lead, overturned the French and pursued the remnants in a mad gallop for several miles; whereupon Lallemand's reserve counter-charged the disorganised British and drove them back in complete disorder, with the loss of 166 men. Slade's absurd reports served only to heighten Wellington's wrath.

The second incident occurred at Campo Mayor (25 March 1811), when Robert Long, in command of the cavalry of Beresford's army, was pursuing French forces which were withdrawing to the fortress of Badajoz. Covering the withdrawal of a train of heavy artillery from Campo Mayor, the French general Latour-Maubourg drew up a small mixed force; Long, who had a light and a heavy brigade, determined to drive off the French cavalry and then fall upon the infantry. He deployed his light brigade into line, $2\frac{1}{2}$ squadrons of 13th Light Dragoons in the centre and Portuguese squadrons on the flanks, but before he could act the 13th was charged by Latour-Mauboug's single cavalry regiment, the 26th Dragoons. After a furious combat the French fled, with the 13th in pell-mell pursuit; unable to stop them, Long sent two Portuguese squadrons after them to act as a reserve, but they merely joined in the chase. When the three remaining Portuguese squadrons bolted when fired upon, Beresford came up and ordered the heavy brigade to hold off, believing that the entire light brigade had been destroyed. Long claimed that Beresford's action prevented him from annihilating the entire French force; in reality, it probably saved the heavy brigade from a mauling.

Meanwhile, the 13th Light Dragoons and the following Portuguese raced on for no less than seven miles. Four miles from the start they overtook the French artillery train, drove off the escort and captured all 16 guns. The Portuguese cut loose many

of the horses and began to lead them back to the Anglo-Portuguese army, to secure the prize-money for captured mounts, but instead of attempting to remove the captured guns the 13th careered on for another three miles, until stopped by fire from the guns of Badajoz. As French troops sallied out from there the disorganised 13th had to gallop back the way they had come, leaving the artillery to be re-possessed by the French, and thus sacrificing completely what could have been a great success.

This action aroused Wellington's condign fury, writing to Beresford on 30 March: 'I wish you would call together the officers of the dragoons, and point out to them the mischiefs which must result from the disorder of the troops in action. The undisciplined ardour of the 13th dragoons ... is not of the description of the determined bravery and steadiness of soldiers confident in their discipline and in their officers. Their conduct was that of a rabble, galloping as fast as their horses could carry them over a plain, after an enemy to whom they could do no mischief when they were broken ... sacrificing substantial advantages, and all the objects of your operation, by their want of discipline ... If the 13th dragoons are again guilty of this conduct, I shall take their horses from them, and send the officers and men to do duty at Lisbon ...'

It is a measure of the tactical awareness of the army, however, that Napier remarked of the 13th's severe reprimand that 'the unsparing admiration of the whole army consoled them!' The account of an

The tactical importance of trumpeters is illustrated in this print of Waterloo, showing the Marquess of Anglesey with his A.D.C. *and orderly trumpeter, presumably sounding the recall after a successful charge. (Engraving by R. Havell after I.M. Wright)*

officer who participated (published in *The Courier*, 20 April 1811) similarly shows a complete lack of understanding of what was required: 'The 13th behaved most nobly. I saw so many instances of individual bravery, as raised my opinion of mankind in general many degrees. The French certainly are fine and brave soldiers, but the superiority of our English horses, and more particularly the superiority of swordsmanship our fellows showed, decided every contest in our favour; it was absolutely like a game at *prison bars*, which you must have seen at school . . . The whole way across the plain was a succession of individual contests, here and there, as the cavalry dispersed . . . it was certainly most beautiful . . .'

Despite the Peninsular experience, the old habit of charging without check occurred again at Waterloo, accounts of which are probably too well known to be repeated here.

In summation, the British cavalry during the period formed a vital part of the military system; equally, they were perhaps not as effective overall as the calibre of the individuals might have suggested. Wellington remarked in 1813 that 'Our cavalry never gained a battle yet. When the infantry have beaten the French, then the cavalry, if they can act, make the whole complete, and do wonders . . .' An equally fair summary was published in the *United Service Journal* in 1831 by an author identified as 'AG': that despite a tendency 'to be carried away by their eagerness in pursuit'. 'If our cavalry did not act so prominent a part in the decision of general battles, and the destruction of beaten armies . . . this failure must be ascribed to other causes than inferiority in the troops. It is sufficient to refer to the actions of that cavalry, when led by a Paget . . . to be convinced that it was capable of any achievement. But the Duke of Wellington was averse to risk his cavalry (never sufficiently numerous), on account of the difficulty of replacing any serious loss in that description of force; and under some officers, who were most unaccountably entrusted with commands, it would have been worse than folly to expect vigour or enterprise'.

COMMANDERS

Only a few British cavalry generals were officers of real talent. Principal among these was Stapleton Cotton, later Viscount Combermere, who from 1810 (apart from two periods of leave) was Wellington's senior cavalry commander in the Peninsula. Having served principally in the light cavalry, he had campaign experience in the Netherlands, the Cape and India, was both capable and intelligent, and Wellington's preferred choice. Wellington requested him as cavalry commander in the Waterloo campaign, but was overruled by the Duke of York; but returning to India, Combermere enjoyed success in independent command. He commanded the cavalry at the time of the decisive charge at Salamanca,

Cavalry combat: the famous pugilist John Shaw of the 2nd Life Guards at Waterloo. By this date the Household Cavalry's original maned helmet had been replaced by one with a woollen caterpillar crest.

Sir John Elley as an officer of the Royal Horse Guards, a portrait which shows the exaggerated proportions of the cavalry bicorn. Elley was one of the most famous examples of a man who rose to high rank having enlisted originally as a private soldier.

Stapleton Cotton, later Lord Combermere; an early portrait, presumably in the uniform of the 25th Light Dragoons (the regimental inscription on the label above the peak of the helmet is partially obscured).

executed by a potentially great commander, John Gaspard Le Marchant, a most intelligent officer whose work at the Royal Military College at High Wycombe immeasurably improved the training of officers, and who was the architect of the cavalry's sword-exercise. His death in this charge deprived the army of one of its most valuable members.

Henry William Paget, later Earl of Uxbridge and Marquess of Anglesey, performed well in command of the cavalry in the Corunna campaign, and was cavalry commander in the Walcheren expedition, but was unemployed in the later Peninsular War due largely to mutual antipathy with Wellington, Paget having eloped with Wellington's sister-in-law. When appointed as cavalry commander in the Waterloo campaign, the attributes which had brought him success with smaller commands proved something of a handicap when leading larger formations, notably his reckless bravery in leading from the front. On the

retreat from Quatre Bras, for example, he took command of two horse artillery guns and, to the despair of their officer (Cavalié Mercer), almost took them and himself into a trap, narrowly evading capture. As he admitted himself, at Waterloo he erred in charging with his first line, and was thus unavailable when needed to control the reserve from following injudiciously.

Such bravery and over-enthusiasm could hardly explain the actions of other cavalry commanders who, for political reasons, Wellington was unable to dismiss until the end of the Peninsular War. Sir William Erskine, for example, was acknowledged to be a madman; when Wellington queried his appointment he was informed officially that 'in his lucid intervals he is an uncommonly clever fellow; and I trust he may have no fit during the campaign, though he looked a little wild before he embarked'. His insanity would seem to be proven when he was killed after throwing himself out of a window in Lisbon. Erskine was also extremely short-sighted, like the German Baron George von Bock, commander of the K.G.L. cavalry, who before making his celebrated charge at Garcia Hernandez had to ask to be pointed in the direction of the enemy. Robert Ballard Long, who commanded at Campo Mayor, was a well-meaning if inept general who admitted, probably only half in joke, that he would have been better suited planting cabbages.

Probably the worst, however, was Sir John ('Jack') Slade, who in 1811 briefly became cavalry commander by seniority during one of Cotton's absences. Slade was an undoubted incompetent, incapable even of managing his paperwork, who seems to have spared little effort in absenting himself from the scene of the action. He commanded during the reverse at Maguilla, which was probably largely his fault, but his failings had been demonstrated to even greater effect in the Corunna campaign, when he commanded a brigade under Paget. Alexander Gordon of the 15th Hussars recorded some of his escapades. At Sahagun he delayed so long in delivering an absurd harangue (ending in 'Blood and slaughter! March!') that the action was over before his command arrived; at Mayorga he halted his brigade twice, ostensibly to adjust his stirrups, until Paget became so exasperated that he ordered the 10th Hussars' commander to take over and lead the charge. Near Cacabelos Slade abandoned his command to report the approach of the French to Moore, who asked why he was doing the job of carrying his own messages; and as the army reached Corunna he again left his brigade, pleading an upset stomach. Paget's opinion was probably accurate: Gordon records him sending an A.D.C. after Slade, to 'ride after that damned stupid fellow' to ensure that he committed no blunder, an order given within the hearing of many officers and soldiers, which can hardly have enhanced Slade's reputation among his brigade!

The failings of such incompetents, however, tend to detract from the reputation of the other cavalry commanders who, if not tacticians of the first rank, carried out their duties earnestly and in some cases with marked distinction; but defects of leadership do help to explain the sometimes mediocre results of cavalry actions.

THE PLATES

A: Training: sword exercises, c. 1805

In this plate a corporal of the 16th Light Dragoons instructs three troopers in the sword exercise, c. 1805; the uniform is that introduced from 1796. Three 'cuts' are demonstrated: 'front give point', ready to strike forwards; 'left give point', striking down and to the left; and 'horse near-side protect', to parry a blow. When performed on foot, the left arm was held to represent its position holding the reins when mounted. Even such drill was not without hazards: so little was the army regarded in certain quarters that when a party of the 10th Light Dragoons began to perform the sword-exercise at Leatherhead Fair in October 1803, the crowd took it as being provocative and a severe affray ensued, in which serious injuries were sustained on both sides.

B: Heavy Cavalry

These plates depict the equipment of heavy cavalry regiments. The main figures show the heavy cavalry uniform worn from 1796 to 1812, with the blue facings and yellow lace of the 1st (Royal) Dragoons, and the same with white lace worn by the 2nd (Royal North British) Dragoons. The ten-inch 'queue' or pigtail was worn from 1796, replacing the earlier 'club', until 1808 when hair was cut short. Detail illustrations are identified by the numbers which follow:

(1) 1812 pattern dragoon helmet with leather skull, metal fittings and horsehair mane; regimental identification was usually carried on a plaque above the peak. (2) shoulder belt with the 1788 sabre, which was replaced by the waist belt (3), shown here with the 1796 pattern heavy cavalry sabre and the sabretache introduced from 1812; (4) is a typical waist-belt plate, of the King's Dragoon Guards. Examples of the plates worn earlier upon officers' shoulder-belts are (5), (6) and (7), of the 1st, 3rd and 4th Dragoon Guards respectively. (8) shows the 1788 heavy cavalry sabre: 39 in. blade, iron hilt with fish-skin grip bound with brass wire, black leather scabbard with iron chape and throat-locket with frog-hook. (9) shows the construction of the 1796 heavy cavalry sabre, the hilt modified by the removal of the langets: iron hilt and scabbard, black leather-covered grip, 35 in. blade with hatchet tip, later ground to a spear point in some cases. (10) 1796 officers' dress sword: 32 in. blade, black leather scabbard, gilded fittings and silver wire grip. (11) 1796 style sabre presumed to be a regimental pattern of the Household Cavalry, with brass hilt and scabbard. (12) Household Cavalry officers' dress sabre: 35/39 in. blade, gilded fittings and scabbard, black fishskin scabbard-inserts and grip, bound with gilt wire; some examples have a cylindrical pommel, and quillon removed. (13) 1796 pattern officers' sabre, with voided steel guard and black leather or fish-skin grip bound with gilt wire. (14) Heavy Dragoon carbine with 42 in. barrel, carried until the adoption of the 1796 pattern, or until the barrel-length was reduced; (15) shows the fitting for suspension from the belt. (16) flintlock mechanism; (17) flints for carbine and pistol, and cartridges. (18) 1796 pattern carbine with 26 in. barrel; (19) the same fitted with Nock's enclosed lock, some of which had semi-circular projections shielding the side of the priming-pan. (20) Heavy dragoon pistol with 12 in. barrel, an earlier pattern which remained in use at least until the end of the 18th century. (21) 1796 pattern pistol with 9 in. barrel and no provision for the ramrod.

C: 10th Hussars in camp, 1815

This illustration shows a scene in the camp of the 10th Hussars, as might have occurred during the 'Hundred Days' campaign. The men of the 10th wear the uniform with dark blue facings introduced in 1814, and their soft cloth forage caps in place of the dress shako (left). Visiting the camp is a trooper of the 2nd Dragoons, wearing that regiment's distinctive

Left: A memorial to three Waterloo heroes at Cossall, Nottinghamshire: John Shaw and Richard Waplington of the 2nd Life Guards, and Thomas Wheatley of the 23rd Light Dragoons. Only the latter returned home: both the Life Guards fell at Waterloo.

Right: Drills and inspections took up much of the soldier's day, even on campaign; this typical scene shows troop-officers about to inspect a troop, drawn up in two ranks, the usual formation. (Engraving by and after Howitt, published 1798)

forage cap with unique vandycked band. Soldiers' wives and camp-followers accompanied every regiment on campaign, and were always present in camp.

D: 4th Dragoons on the march, c. 1809–11

The rigours of campaign are evident in this Peninsular War scene, showing a column of 4th Dragoons on the march. Although marches usually began in very early morning, the heat of summer was often oppressive, and in dry weather suffocating clouds of dust coated men and horses alike. One officer of the 4th described how the Portuguese climate had bleached both his scarlet jacket and his hair, yet had so tanned the skin that his regiment almost resembled members of the Portuguese army. Uniforms became increasingly dilapidated as the campaign progressed, head-dress and boots warping and clothing becoming ragged and patched; only weapons and harness could be kept in smart condition. In this illustration the officer and sergeant (right) wear 'watering caps', the cavalry undress shako which would be worn with peak folded up or down; their column of weary troopers include some who have replaced their collapsing hats with forage caps.

E: Horse Furniture

This plate illustrates various examples of horse furniture. The figures show a light and heavy dragoon in stable dress, wearing forage caps and plain jackets in blue and red respectively, ornamented only by facing-coloured cuffs and collar patches. The horse furniture illustrated is as follows: (1) heavy cavalry saddlery and equipment as used on campaign, the valise bearing the identification of the King's Dragoon Guards. (2) horse furniture of a trooper of the 13th Light Dragoons, 1812, from a print by Charles Hamilton Smith. A folded blanket takes the place of the sharabraque; for some regiments the sheepskin saddle cover had a coloured cloth edging. The 'bucket' at the right front accommodated the carbine muzzle. (3) typical full dress furniture, of an officer of the 4th (Queen's own) Dragoons, from a painting by Reinagle. The shabraque and holster caps (which were often facing-coloured, unlike this example) usually bore a regimental badge in the rear corners and on the holster caps; only the latter are present in this case, the insignia is the reversed 'C' cypher of Queen Charlotte. The bridle includes a white head-collar, which for service was often of the

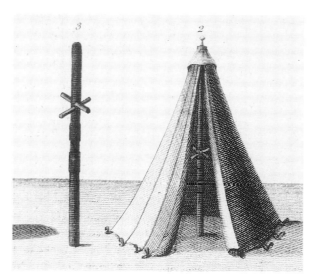

Contemporary engraving of a military bell-tent, occupied in the field by several soldiers, showing in detail the central pole with projecting arms upon which equipment could be hung, or against which firearms could be stacked.

Contemporary engraving of a camp-kitchen, a type usually constructed when camping for more than a single night. A camp-kettle is shown simmering over a fire in one of the cooking-bays, and a woman camp-follower or soldier's wife lights another cook-fire; she wears a typical costume, including apparently an old military jacket and a cut-down cocked hat.

same material as the bridle. (4) officers' full dress furniture of the 15th Hussars, c.1813, from a picture by Hamilton Smith. The large amount of decoration is typical, the 15th adopting harness ornamented with cowrie-shells in 1807. (5) 1805 light cavalry or hussar saddle, with the separate 'pilch' or quilted leather seat. (6) heavy cavalry saddle of the design introduced in 1796; a pistol holster was carried on each side of the pommel, and looped straps held the folded cloak. (7) light cavalry sharabraque of an officer of the 23rd Light Dragoons, c.1812–15, taken from an extant example. (8) valise-ends bearing typical regimental identification for the 1st Royal Dragoons (b) and 15th King's Hussars (a), and the individual troop numbers sometimes borne on the opposite end of the valise: this example is shown by Dighton, opposite the 'R.N.B.D.' on the 2nd Dragoons' valise (c).

F: Light Cavalry

The figure to the left (26) shows a sergeant of the 10th Light Dragoons, 1790, after a painting by George Stubbs. The Tarleton helmet bears the regimental insignia of the Prince of Wales's crest; other sources show it positioned lower on the skull. The facing-coloured plume and turban were altered by the late 1790s to a white plume with red base, and a blue or black turban for all regiments. The sleeveless 'shell' was worn over the short jacket from 1784 to 1796, but was omitted in some orders of dress, for example for drill. Rank insignia was of regimental devising at this period, in this case two facing-coloured sleeve chevrons and a sash with blue and white edges. The figures at right depict the 1812 light dragoon uniform, including a shako and Polish-style jacket, with the buff facings and yellow lace of the 13th Light Dragoons (27) and the orange facings and white lace of the 14th (28). The pouch was supported on narrow straps attached to the inside of the carbine belt; for officers, the dress sabretache had an ornamented front and was suspended on three slings instead of the two of the other ranks. Detail illustrations are as follows: (1) 2.5 in. wide shoulder belts supporting the pouch (which was white leather until 1793, black thereafter), and 1788 light cavalry sabre. Plates borne on the shoulder belt were generally discontinued by the late 1790s, but some continued in use with the auxiliary forces; examples illustrated here are officers' plates of (2) 7th Light Dragoons, (3) 15th Light Dragoons and

'The first lesson': although post-dating the Napoleonic Wars, this scene is typical of a regimental riding-school, the students wearing undress uniform. The finished product, with a proper cavalryman's 'seat', is inset. (Print after Harry and Arthur Payne)

(4) London and Westminster Light Horse Volunteers, and (5) an other ranks' plate of the 14th Light Dragoons. (6) shows the rear of a Tarleton helmet of the 16th Light Dragoons, with the hair-dressing termed a 'club'. (7) tropical helmet of the 20th Light Dragoons, bearing the alligator badge of Jamaica, from the period when the regiment bore the title of that island. (8) 1788 pattern light cavalry sabre: 36 in. blade, iron hilt with ribbed black leather grip, iron scabbard with wooden inserts covered with black leather. (9) 1796 pattern light cavalry sabre: 33 in. blade, iron hilt and scabbard, black leather-covered grip; this version has the langets removed, a common modification. (10) officers' version of the 1796 pattern; the blade often bore blued and gilded decoration, and the grip was bound with brass or gilt wire. This version retains the original langets. (11) officers' sabre, used from 1788 until c.1801 by some regiments; examples are recorded with the insignia of the 7th, 10th, 21st, and 30th Light Dragoons on the

langets. Iron hilt, chequered ebony grip, 32 in. blade, iron scabbard with black leather inserts; that illustrated bears the Prince of Wale's crest of the 10th Light Dragoons on the langnet. (12) 10th Light Dragoons officers' pattern which succeeded that shown in (11); 32 in. blade, gilded hilt with fish-skin grip bound with gilt wire, brass scabbard and silver Prince of Wale's crest on the langets. (13) officer's non-regulation sabre of 'mameluke' design, taken from an example used by an officer of the 20th Light Dragoons; 32 in. curved blade, ebony grip, steel cross-guard. (14) Elliott carbine with 28 in. barrel. (15) suspension-bar of 1796 carbonc. (16) Baker rifled carbine with 20/21 in. barrel and scrolled brass trigger guard, taken from a weapon marked to the 7th Light Dragoons. The so-called 'pistol butt' used by the 10th had a wooden projection conforming approximately to the shape of the brass guard illustrated. (17) Paget carbine with 16 in. barrel, bolt lock and later type of reinforced cock and swivel ramrod; (18) shows the Paget suspension-bar. (19) 1796 pistol modified to take a ramrod, fitted with Nock's enclosed lock (20). (21) Light Dragoon pistol with 9 in. barrel, with iron ramrod and later style of reinforced cock. (22) modified Light Dragoon pistol, with shortened stock capped with a brass end, to permit the fitting of a swivel ramrod. (23) picker and brush used for cleaning a flintlock. (24) hussar officer's pouch, and (25) silver plated plug-in spur, both taken from extant examples.

G: Assembly in line

This shows a regiment of dragoons assembled in line, each squadron of two troops in two ranks, in 'close order' (3 feet 6 inches between ranks), the frontage depending upon the strength. In 'loose files' there was a six-inch gap between each trooper, giving a frontage of 34 inches per man; in 'close files' the trooper's knees touched those of the man on either side, and in 'open files' there was a horse-breadth between each man. Officers (shown here on light bay horses) occupied the ends of each squadron's front rank, another carried the squadron standard (not usually taken on campaign), and each squadron commander was one horse-length in front of the standard. Two horse-lengths behind the rear rank were the supernumerary officers, sergeants and quartermasters, with the farriers (not shown here), when present, a further horse-length behind them. The trumpeters (shown here on grey horses) were not mentioned in the regulations, except that some rode with the supernumeraries; one is shown here with each squadron commander, and one with the commanding officer at the head of the line.

H: Brigade tactics

This depicts the ideal method of a brigade advancing. The first line, in echelon of squadrons, is preceded about 150 yards ahead by two lines of skirmishers, one in reserve behind the leading skirmish-line. About 400–500 yards behind the first line of squadrons is the second, either halted or following at a walk. The same distance behind them is the reserve, halted in column of half squadrons, ready to exploit a breakthrough or cover a retreat, with sufficient space between the squadrons to permit them to move into line without difficulty, and to allow retiring elements of the first two lines to pass through them. This view is somewhat simplified, as units might advance in half squadrons, engaging whatever targets presented themselves.

I: Capture of the 'Eagle', Waterloo

One of the most celebrated incidents involving a British cavalryman at this period was the capture of the 'Eagle' of the French 45th Line at Waterloo, by Sergeant Charles Ewart of the 2nd Dragoons (Scots Greys). This took place during the Union Brigade's

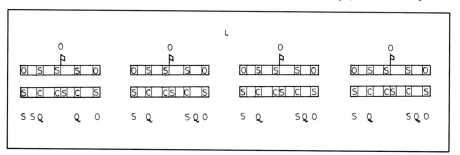

A regiment formed in line in close order, showing the positions taken up by officers (O), sergeants (S), corporals (C), quartermasters (Q) and lieutenant-colonel in command (L). The officers in front of each squadron's standard were the squadron-commanders.

Pvt. Samuel Godley of the 2nd Life Guards unhorsed at Waterloo, executing a parry with the sabre. This man was nicknamed 'The Marquess of Granby' due to his bald head; he killed the French cuirassier, mounted his horse and rejoined his regiment.

A dismounted Life Guardsman fighting a Cuirassier whom he slew

counter-attack against d'Erlon's Corps at about 2.00 p.m. During his regiment's advance Ewart came upon the 'Eagle' of the 45th and its escort and, in his own words, 'had a hard contest for it', settled when he cut down the officer who bore it. A second Frenchman he cut through the teeth; and, parrying a bayonet-thrust, dispatched a third with a cut through the head, before riding to the rear with his trophy. This deed earned him considerable fame and a commission in the 5th Royal Veteran Battalion. Illustrated is the equipment for active service, including a forage net and rolled cloak over the front of the saddle, waterdeck wrapped around the valise, and a grain sack at the right rear of the saddle. The valise bore on its right end 'R/NB/D' ('Royal North British Dragoons'), and Dighton's painting of the exploit shows personal and troop identification numbers on the left end, Ewart's being shown as 'B/N:3'. The unique regimental bearskin cap is enclosed in a waterproof cover.

Bibliography and further reading

For details of uniform, equipment and use, the following are recommended:

Barthorp, M., *British Cavalry Uniforms since 1660*, Poole, 1984

Blackmore, H.L., *British Military Firearms 1650–1850*, London 1961

Chappell, M., *British Cavalry Equipments 1800–1941*, London 1983 (Osprey Men-at-Arms series no. 138)

Fosten, B., *Wellington's Heavy Cavalry*, London 1982 (MAA series no. 130)

Fosten, B., *Wellington's Light Cavalry*, London 1982 (MAA series no. 126)

Mollo, J., *Waterloo Uniforms: British Cavalry*, London 1973

Robson, B., *Swords of the British Army*, London 1975 (standard work on the subject)

Strachan, H., *British Military Uniforms 1768–96*,

London 1975 (extracts from official regulations and inspection returns)

Tylden, G., *Horses and Saddlery*, London 1975 (the best work on these neglected subjects)

The following accounts by cavalrymen of the period are recommended:

Bragge, W., *Peninsular Portrait: The Letters of Capt. William Bragge*, ed. S.A.C. Cassells, London 1963 (3rd Dragoons)

Brotherton, T., *A Hawk at War: The Peninsular Reminiscences of General Sir Thomas Brotherton*, ed. B. Perrett, Chippenham 1986 (14th Light Dragoons)

Cocks, Hon. E.C., *Intelligence Officer in the Peninsula: Letters and Diaries of Major Hon. Edward Charles Cocks*, ed. J.V. Page, Tunbridge Wells 1986 (16th Light Dragoons: one of the most intelligent and capable officers in the army)

Gordon, A., *Journal of a Cavalry Officer in the Corunna Campaign*, ed. H.C. Wylly, London 1913 (15th Light Dragoons)

Gray, E.A., *The Trumpet of Glory: The Military Career of John Shipp, first Veterinary Surgeon to join the British Army*, London 1985 (23rd Light Dragoons)

Hawker, P., *Journal of a Regimental Officer during the Recent Campaign in Portugal and Spain*, London 1810 (14th Light Dragoons)

James, H., *Surgeon James's Journal 1815*, ed. J. Vansittart, London 1964 (1st Life Guards)

Landsheit, N., *The Hussar: The Story of Norbert Landsheit*, ed. G.R. Gleig, London 1837 (York Hussars and 20th Light Dragoons)

Lunt, J., *Scarlet Lancer*, London 1964 (biography of John Luard, 16th Light Dragoons)

Tomkinson, W., *Diary of a Cavalry Officer*, ed. J. Tomkinson, London 1895 (16th Light Dragoons: a classic memoir)

Verner, W., *Reminiscences of William Verner*, ed. R.W. Verner, London 1965 (Society for Army Historical Research Special Publication) (7th Hussars)

Vivian, Lord, *Memoir and Letters*, ed. Hon. C. Vivian, London 1897 (7th Hussars)

Woodberry, G., *Journal of Lieutenant Woodberry in the Campaigns of 1813–15*, Paris 1896 (18th Hussars)

Table E: The soldier's equipment

Provided by the colonel (i.e. at government expense)
Sleeved cloak every 12 years; pair iron-shod boots every 6 years; pair gloves annually.
Heavy cavalry: one hat annually; coat, waistcoat, pair breeches every two years.
Light cavalry: upper jacket, under jacket, flannel waistcoat, pair leather breeches every two years; helmet every three years; undress (watering) cap every four years.
Equipment
Accoutrements to last 20 years: pouch for 30 rounds with straps and buckles with two brass tongues; carbine belt (3 ins. wide for heavy, $2\frac{1}{2}$ ins. for light cavalry) with brass buckles, slider and swivel; sword waist-belt ($2\frac{1}{2}$ ins. wide for heavy, $1\frac{1}{4}$ ins. for light cavalry) with brass plate and slide, and bar with double tongue; buff leather bayonet frog and sword knot.
Horse furniture
To last 16 years, saddle with web girth, stirrups with leathers and buckles, holster and shoe-case with straps, holster cover, carbine bucket with strap and picket ring.
To last 12 years: bit.
To last 6 years: bridoon, reins, nose band, martingale, breast strap, surcingles, crupper, with buckles; double and single forage straps with buckles, double and single cloak straps with buckles, carbine strap with buckle, horse collar with iron chain, leather cloak-cover.
'*Necessaries*' provided at each soldier's own expense, renewed when necessary
Pair breeches, pair braces, stable jacket, stable trousers, forage cap, 3 shirts, night cap, stock and clasp, 3 pairs worsted stockings, pair long gaiters, 2 pairs shoes with pair buckles, 3 shoe brushes, 2 combs, razor, soap, clothes brush, picker and worm (for firearms), button stick and hook, powder bag, powder puff and powder, emery, oil, pipe-clay, blacking, waterproof case for carbine lock, and horse-equipment: nose bag, watering bridle, mane-comb, sponge, curry-comb, brush, scissors and pair of saddle-bags.
(The above is from Charles James' *The Regimental Companion*, London 1804, but minor differences may be found in other contemporary sources; in the 2nd Dragoon Guards, for example, regimental 'necessaries' included an extra shirt, 2 pocket handkerchiefs, and a rosette and 'clubbing-iron' for the man's hair-dressing).

'The Girl I Left Behind Me': light dragoons taking leave of their sweethearts on their departure for active service. Although this engraving by Bartolozzi after Bunbury presents a somewhat sentimentalized view, such scenes were commonplace and very emotional, for relatives left at home might wait many years for news of their menfolk; as described by John Mayne's poem Mary Marton (published 1807): 'Fond Mary, the while, in her spirits quite broken,/ Disturb'd in her sleep, and perplex'd in her mind,/No letters from William, no tidings, no token . . .'

Camp scenes. The top row depicts ordinary soldiers' tents, with the wooden internal frame; at the right are 'fly tents' with a canvas 'fly' at the top. The middle row shows an officer's tent (left), and at right a larger tent for the accommodation of a number of men, who slept on either side of the side-opening. The bottom row shows 'marquis' tents (i.e. marquees), of larger size and with a chimney constructed, when camping at the same place for some time. (Engraving after N.C. Goodnight)

Works concerning cavalry generals include:

Anglesey, Marquess of, *One Leg: The Life and Letters of Henry William Paget, First Marquess of Anglesey*, London 1961

Combermere, Lord, *Life and Correspondence of Field-Marshal Lord Combermere*, ed. Viscountess Combermere & W. Knollys, London 1866

Long, R.B., *Peninsular Cavalry General: The Correspondence of Lt.Gen. Robert Ballard Long*, ed. T.H. McGuffie, London 1951

Thoumine, R.H., *Scientific Soldier: A Life of General Le Marchant*, London 1968

In addition to ordinary regimental histories, the following concern the period exclusively:

Clark-Kennedy, A.E., *Attack the Colour: The Royal Dragoons in the Peninsula and at Waterloo*, London 1975

Mann, M., *And They Rode On: The King's Dragoon Guards at Waterloo*, Salisbury 1984

An interesting study of barracks is 'Early Cavalry Barracks in Great Britain', C.R.B. Barrett, in *The Cavalry Journal*, VII (1912), pp. 161–76

Regimental transport: all regiments maintained their own transport-waggons for carrying their baggage, often hired civilian vehicles. It was common for these to be as overloaded as shown here, and consequently they were considerably dangerous: for example, one belonging to the Royal Horse Guards overturned going down a hill near Wellingborough in June 1801, killing one of the women riding on it and injuring two others. (Engraving after W.H. Pyne)

Formations and drill are covered in the Fosten and Mollo titles listed above, and of many contemporary manuals perhaps the most useful is the official one, *Instructions and Regulations for the Formations and Movements of the Cavalry*, 1796, which appeared in a number of editions (4th edn. London 1801)

For the general history of the British Army of the period, see:

Fortescue, Hon. Sir J., *History of the British Army*, Vols. IV–X, London 1906–20

Glover, M., *Wellington as Military Commander*, London 1968

Glover, M., *Wellington's Army in the Peninsula*, Newton Abbot 1977

Glover, R., *Peninsular Preparation: the Reform of the British Army 1795–1809*, Cambridge 1963

Haythornthwaite, P.J., *Wellington's Military Machine*, Tunbridge Wells, 1989

Oman, Sir C.W.C., *History of the Peninsular War*, Oxford 1902–30

Oman, Sir C.W.C., *Wellington's Army*, London 1912

Rogers, H.C.B., *Wellington's Army*, London 1979

For details of regimental insignia, see:

Buckell, L.E., 'Metal Regimental Badges on Light Cavalry Helmets', *Journal of the Society for Army Historical Research*, Vol. XX, 1941.

Parkyn, H.G., *Shoulder-Belt Plates and Buttons*, Aldershot 1956

Notes sur les planches en couleur

A Un caporal des 16èmes Dragons Légers instruit les cavaliers dans le maniement de l'épée. On démontre trois 'coups' différents.

B Uniforme de cavalerie lourde avec les parements bleus et la dentelle jaune des 1ers Dragons (Royal). Les 2nds Dragons (Royal North British) portaient le même uniforme avec de la dentelle blanche. **B1** Casque de dragons de modèle 1812. **B2** Ceinture en bandoulière avec le sabre de 1788. **B3** Sabre et sabretache de cavalerie lourde de modèle 1796. **B4** Plaque de ceinture des King's Dragoon Guards. Exemples de plaques portées auparavant sur les ceintures en bandoulière des officiers en **B5**, **B6** et **B7** dans les 1ers, 3èmes et 4èmes Dragoon Guards respectivement. **B8** Sabre de cavalerie lourde de 1788. **B9** sabre de cavalerie lourde de 1796. **B10** Epée de parade des officiers en 1796. **B11** Sabre de style 1796 avec garde et fourreau en cuivre. **B12** Sabre de parade des officiers de la Garde à cheval. **B13** Sabre d'officier modèle 1796. **B14** Carabine de dragons lourds avec baril de 42 pouces. **B15** Mécanisme de suspension à la ceinture. **B16** Mécanisme de platine à pierre. **B17** Pierre pour carabine et pistolet, cartouches. **B18** Carabine de 1796 avec baril de 26 pouces. **B19** La même, équipée de la platine fermée de Nock. **B20** Pistolet de dragons lourds avec baril de 12 pouces. **B21** Pistolet de modèle 1796 avec baril de 9 pouces.

C Une scène de campement. Les uniformes ont des parements bleu foncé, les calots en drap souples sont portés à la place du shako de parade. Un cavalier des 2èmes dragons visite le camp. Il porte un calot avec une bande dentelée.

D Scène de la guerre de la péninsule ibérique où figure une colonne de 4èmes dragons en marche. L'officier et le sergeant (à droite) portent des 'watering caps', sorte de shakos.

E Les figures montrent un dragon léger et un dragon lourd en uniforme d'écurie avec calot et veste simple bleue et rouge respectivement avec des manchettes et des écussons de col de la couleur des parements. **E1** Sellerie et matériel de cavalerie lourde. **E2** Harnais d'un cavalier des 13èmes Dragons Légers, 1812. **E3** Harnais d'apparat typique d'un officier des 4èmes Dragons (ceux de la Reine). La bride comporte un collier blanc. **E4** Harnais d'apparat des officiers des 15èmes Hussards, 1813 environ. **E5** Cavalerie légère ou selle de hussard avec 'pilch' séparé, sorte de siège en cuir capitonné. **E6** Selle de cavalerie lourde. Un étui à revolver était suspendu de chaque côté du pommeau. **E7** Sharabraque de cavalerie légère d'un officier des 23èmes Dragons Légers, autour de 1812–15. **E8** Extrémités du sac de voyage portant l'identification régimentale typique des 1ers Dragons Royaux et des 15èmes Hussards du Roi.

F La figure sur la gauche représente un sergeant des 10èmes Dragons Légers, 1790. L'insigne de rang comporte deux chevrons de manche de la couleur des parements et une ceinture à bord bleu et rouge. Les figures de droite représentent l'uniforme des dragons légers de 1812, y compris un shako et une veste de style polonais. **F1** Ceintures en bandoulière de 6cm de large soutenant une bourse et sabre de cavalerie légère de 1788. Exemples de plaques d'officiers des: **F2** 7èmes Dragons Légers, **F3** 15èmes Dragons Légers et **F4** London and Westminster Light Horse Volunteers. **F5** Les 14èmes Dragons Légers. **F6** Arrière d'un casque Tarleton des 16èmes Dragons Légers. **F7** Casque tropical des 20èmes Dragons Légers avec badge alligator de la Jamaïque. **F8** Sabre de cavalerie légère de modèle 1788. **F9** Sabre de cavalerie légère de modèle 1796. **F10** Version officiers du modèle 1796 (avec languettes). **F11** Sabre d'officier, utilisé de 1788 jusqu'à 1801 environ. **F14** Carabine Elliot avec baril 28 pouces. **F15** Barre de suspension de carabine 1796. **F16** Carabine-fusil Baker avec baril de 20/21 pouces et pontet ern cuivre étamé. **F17** Carabine Paget avec baril de 16 pouces, fermoir de culasse et style plus tardif de chien renforcé. **F18** Barre de suspension Paget. **F19** Pistolet de 1796 modifié pour accepter une baguette. **F20** Pistolet avec platine fermée de Nock. **F21** Pistolet de dragon léger avec baril de 9 pouces. **F22** Pistolet de dragon léger modifié avec monture raccourcie terminée par un embout en cuivre. **F23** Grattoir et brosse utilisés pour nettoyer une platine à pierre. **F24** Bourse d'un officier des hussards. **F25** Eperon en métal argenté æmmancher.

G Régiment de dragons assemblé en ligne, chaque escadron de deux troupes en deux rangs. Les officiers occupent les bouts du premier rang de chaque escadron, à une longueur de cheval devant l'étendard.

H Avancement de brigade idéal: la première ligne est précédée de deux lignes de

Farbtafeln

A Ein Korporal des Leichten Dragoner-Regiments Nr.16 unterrichtet Soldaten im Säbelfechten; drei verschiedene Manöver werden gezeigt.

B Kavallerieuniform des (Royal) Dragoner-Regiments Nr.1 mit blauen Aufschlägen und gelben Litzen; dieselbe mit weißen Litzen wurde vom (Royal North British) Dragoner-Regiment Nr.2 getragen. **B1** Dragonerhelm von 1812. **B2** Schulterriemen mit Säbel von 1788. **B3** Säbel und Säbeltasche der schweren Kavallerie von 1796. **B4** Gürtelplatte der King's Dragonergarde. **B5**, **B6** und **B7** zeigen früher von Offizieren getragene Schulterriemenplatten des 1, 3 und 4 Dragoner-Garderegiments. **B8** Säbel der schweren Kavallerie von 1788, und **B9** von 1796. **B10** Gala-Säbel eines Offiziers von 1796. **B11** Säbel von 1796, mit Heft und Scheide aus Bronze. **B12** Gala-Säbel der Gardekavallerie-Offiziere **B13** Offizierssäbel von 1796. **B14** Karabiner der schweren Dragoner mit 1,06m langem Lauf. **B15** Riemenzeug für Aufhängung am Gürtel. **B16** Steinschloß-Mechanismus. **B17** Feuersteine für Karabiner und Pistole samt Patronen. **B18** Karabiner von 1796 mit 66cm-Lauf, und **B19** mit verkapseltem Nock-Schloß. **B20** Pistole der schweren Dragoner mit 304mm-Lauf. **B21** Pistole von 1796 mit 228mm-Lauf.

C Eine Lagerszene. Uniformen mit dunkelblauen Auschlägen, Schiffchen aus weichem Stoff werden anstatt der Tschakos getragen. Das Lager wird von einem Soldaten des 2. Dragoner-Regiments besucht, mit Schiffchen mit Van-Dyke-Band.

D Szene aus dem Halbinselkrieg mit einer Abteilung des 4. Dragoner-Regiments in Marsch. Der Offizier und der Sergeant (rechts) tragen sog. 'Watering Caps' (geflammte Kappen?).

E Die Figuren zeigen eine leichten und einen schweren Dragoner in Stalluniform, mit Schiffchen und einfarbigen blauen, bezw. roten Jacken mit Manschetten und Kragenabzeichen in der Farbe der Aufschläge. **E1** Sattelzeug und Geräte der schweren Kavallerie. **E2** Pferdezeug eines Soldaten des 13. Leichtdragoner-Regiments, 1812. **E3** Typisches Gala-Pferdezeug eines Offiziers des 4. (Queen's own) Dragoner-Regiments. Zaumzeug mit weiß eingefaßtem Kragenstück. **E4** Gala Pferdezeug eines Offiziers des 15. Husaren-Regiments, ca. 1813. **E5** Leichter Kavallerie- oder Husarensattel, mit separatem 'Pilch', einem gepolsterten Ledersitz. **E6** Schwerer Kavalleriesattel; Pistolenhalfter wurde zu beiden Seiten des Sattelknaufs getragen. **E7** Kavellerie-Schabracke eines Offiziers des 23. Leichtdragoner-Regiments, ca. 1812–15. **E8** Tornisterenden zeigen typische Regimentskennzeichen für das 1. königliche Dragoner- und das 15. Königshusaren-Regiment.

F Die Figur links zeigt einen Sergeanten des 10. Leichtdragoner-Regiments, 1790. Rangabzeichen sind zwei Ärmelwinkel in Farbe der Aufschläge und eine Schärpe mit blauweißen Rändern. Die Figuren rechts die Leichtdragoner-Uniform von 1812 mit Tschako und mit Jacke in polnischem Stil. **F1** Schulterriemen, 63mm breit, tragen einen Ranzen und die leichten Kavalleriesäbel von 1788; Beispiele von Riemenplatten bei Offizieren der: **F2** 7. Leichtdragoner, **F3** 15. Leichtdragoner und **F4** Westminster Leichtberittenen Freiwilligen. **F5** Die 14. Leichtdragoner. **F6** Rückseite eines Tarleton-Helms der 16. Leichtdragoner. **F7** Tropenhelm der 20. Leichtdragoner mit Alligator-Abzeichen von Jamaika. **F8** Säbel der leichten Kavallerie nach Muster von 1788. **F10** Offiziersversion des Säbels von 1796 (mit 'Langets'?). **F11** Offizierssäbel, benutzt von 1788 bis ca. 1801. **F14** Elliott-Karabiner, Lauf 711mm lang. **F15** Hängestab eines Karabiners von 1796. **F16** Baker-Karabiner mit gezogenem Lauf (508/533mm) und verziertem Messing-Abzugsbügel. **F17** Paget-Karabiner mit 400mm-Lauf, Gewehrschloß und verstärktem Hahn in späterem Stil. **F18** Paget-Hängestab. **F19** Pistole von 1796, modifiziert für Ladestock. **F20** Pistole mit verkapseltem Nock-Schloß. **F21** Leichtdragoner-Pistole mit 228mm-Lauf. **F22** Modifizierte Leichtdragoner-Pistole mit verkürztem Kolben mit messingbeschlagenem Ende. **F23** Reinigungsgeräte für Steinschloß. **F24** Ranzen eines Husarenoffiziers. **F25** Versilberter Anstecksporn.

G Dragoner-Regiment in Formation, jedes Schwadron von zwei Truppen in zwei Reihen. Die Offiziere stehen am Ende jeder Schwadron-Vorderreihe, eine Pferdelänge vor der Fahne.

H Idealer Brigaden-Vormarsch: der ersten Reihe gehen zwei Reihen Scharmützler voraus. Rund 400m dahinter folgt die zweite Schwadronsreihe, und hinter ihr die Reserve.

tirailleurs. A 400–500 mètres derrière se trouve la seconde ligne d'escadrons, et derrière eux se trouve la réserve.

I La capture de 'l'Aigle' de la 45ème ligne française à Waterloo. Illustr le matériel de service actif. Comprend un filet àfourrage et un manteau roulé à l'avant de la selle, une bâche enroulée autour du sac de voyage et un sac de grain à l'arrière de la selle. Le sac de voyage porte les lettres 'R/NB/D' ('Royal North British Dragoons').

I Die Erbeutung eines 'Adlers' des französischen 45. Linienregiments bei Waterloo. Hier sieht man die Ausrüstung für den aktiven Dienst, inkl. Vorratsnetz und eingerollten Umhang über der Sattelvorderseite, in wasserdichte Decke eingewickelter Tornister und ein Sack mit Korn an der rechten Sattelrückseite. Der Tornister trägt die Aufschrift 'R/NB/D' (Royal North British Dragoons).